'OVER THE HILLS AND FAR AWAY'

'OVER THE HILLS AND FAR AWAY'

THE LIFE OF
BEATRIX POTTER

MATTHEW DENNISON

PEGASUS BOOKS
NEW YORK LONDON

Over the Hills and Far Away

Pegasus Books Ltd
148 West 37th Street, 13th Floor
New York, NY 10018

First Pegasus Books hardcover edition April 2017

ISBN: 978-1-68177-350-6

10 9 8 7 6 5 4 3 2 1

Printed in the United States of America
Distributed by W. W. Norton & Company, Inc.

For Aeneas, with love

'Ton coucher de soleil, tu l'auras. Je l'exigerai.'

Le Petit Prince,
Antoine de Saint-Exupéry, 1943

'... a theory I have seen – that genius – like murder –
will out – its bent being simply a matter of
circumstance'

Beatrix Potter, *Journal*, 5 June 1891

'She was of strict integrity... a benevolent, charitable,
good woman, and capable of strong attachments...
She had a cultivated mind, and was, generally speaking,
rational and consistent – but she had prejudices
on the side of ancestry'

Jane Austen, *Persuasion*, 1816

Contents

· 1 ·

'Unloved birthplace'

Beatrix at the age of five, dressed 'absurdly' uncomfortably in starched white cotton piqué, like Alice in John Tenniel's illustrations to *Alice's Adventures in Wonderland*.

'Dogs barked; boys whistled in the street; the cook laughed, the parlour maid ran up and down-stairs; and a canary sang like a steam engine'

The Tale of Johnny Town-Mouse, 1918

BEATRIX POTTER was six or seven years old – in this instance she muddled the date – when her father Rupert gave her a sheet of drawings she kept for the rest of her life.

Like Aunt Dorcas and Aunt Porcas in *The Tale of Little Pig Robinson*, Beatrix Potter's parents 'led prosperous un-eventful lives'. Unlike those resourceful sows, they did not support themselves by taking in washing or keeping hens. Before his marriage in 1863, Rupert Potter had qualified as a barrister; his wife Helen Leech received a legacy of £50,000 on her father's death in 1861. From the outset, husband and wife enjoyed the leisurely spoils of a comfortable fortune and cheap domestic help. Both children of dynamic self-made men, they appear to have cherished few ambitions for themselves beyond social gentility. Beatrix described them as apathetic.[1]

Covertly, Rupert Potter craved the gadfly life of the boule-vardier: he was mostly absent from his chambers at 3 New Square, Lincoln's Inn. In instinct, this voluble, opinionated and irritable man remained pontifical until the day he died, 'oppressively well informed' and 'very fidgetty [sic] about things'; his interest in art was genuine.[2] So, too, his love of fishing and his hearty dislike of Liberal premier William Ewart Gladstone. Over time, his absorption in photography eclipsed other enthusiasms; his many photographs of his wife suggest that Helen Potter mistrusted levity.

Art, politics, fishing, photography and Rupert Potter's 'fidgetiness' all played their part in Beatrix Potter's up-bringing. Among Rupert's friends were painter John Everett Millais and Victorian art world supremo Sir Charles Eastlake. For the former he photographed portrait sitters – restless children and a self-dramatising Gladstone – and provided landscape photographs for backgrounds. His purchases on his own behalf included a sepia drawing by Landseer, bought at Christie's for five pounds,[3] and almost thirty of Randolph Caldecott's illustrations for children's rhyme books, for which he paid considerably more. He col-lected letters, including a complaint about Longman the publisher written by a querulous elderly Wordsworth.[4]

The sketches Rupert Potter gave his tow-haired daughter in 1872 or 1873 were of swans and ducks, with a pelican for good measure. They were not his first attempt at drawing waterfowl. Twenty years previously, doodling as a student, he had outlined a flight of ducks skimming over bulrushes. Two wore hats. One, in a poke bonnet fastened with ribbon under the chin, foreshadowed Jemima Puddle-duck. Later Beatrix drew and kept ducks of her own. They emerge from her published work as foolish animals, none more so than Jemima, whom she treated with contempt bordering on cruelty. That Beatrix afterwards kept her father's sketch is characteristic. She came from a family of hoarders; she mythologised aspects of her childhood.

The Potters lived in London. Not for them the 'cosy thatched cottage... in an orchard at the top of a steep red Devonshire lane' of Little Pig Robinson's upbringing, or meagre rented rooms like that in College Court, where Beatrix imagined her Tailor of Gloucester; instead, a smart new Kensington townhouse of lugubrious respectability unleavened by picturesqueness. Its plot, south of Old Brompton Road, had been Mr Pettiward's cherry orchard until 1811; afterwards, nurseryman Philip Conway, of neighbouring Earl's Court, gardened here, in an area once dominated by market gardens and fruit growing. Number 2 Bolton Gardens was one of eight new houses built only in 1862. Among local landmarks was a grove of walnut trees. A generation ago, mulberry trees fruited nearby and five acres were laid down to arable farming, including rye.[5] Over the course of her childhood Beatrix would witness the felling of the last fruit trees and the departure of resident rooks. A diary entry written when she was sixteen recorded 'every patch of land being built upon'.[6]

Surviving photographs show an imposing, unlovely house: nine tall plate-glass windows to the front; massed rectangular stacks of chimneys; a pilastered porch at the side, reached by a flight of steps; to the rear a brick-walled garden similar in size, according to Beatrix, to the pre-historic monument at Stonehenge and, despite criss-cross panels of wooden fencing topping its high walls, much invaded by cats. Hierarchical architecture, notwithstanding its monumental aspect: most austere at the top, on the nursery floor, where the wind howled in the chimneys and sparrows nested under the guttering. As in *The Sly Old Cat*, area steps descended to basement service quarters. Thriftily, Helen Potter had furnished the servants' hall with cast-off dining chairs inherited from her father-in-law. More than once, one of these chairs collapsed.[7]

In the drawing room, aspidistras contributed to an atmosphere of stagnant good behaviour. Bookcases in the same room served a more-than-decorative purpose; in the course of spring-cleaning, the maids invariably – and disconcertingly – rearranged the books.[8] It was not a house for childish high spirits. Feelingly, Beatrix later wrote, 'I think myself that a house that is too small is more comfortable than one a great deal too large', a philosophy she put into practice in the houses that, as an adult, she bought for herself.[9] In her own writing, only one house suggests typical Victorian urban interiors, the 'very beautiful doll's-house' belonging to Lucinda and Jane in *The Tale of Two Bad Mice*. To her editor Beatrix described this doll's house as resembling 'the kind of house where one cannot sit down without upsetting something, I know the sort!';[10] to the reader she describes without censure its devastation at the hands of mice Tom Thumb and Hunca Munca. Throughout her tales, simple domestic tasks – unpacking the vegetable box, shopping for groceries, carving a ham, rolling out pastry, baking a pie, spring-cleaning – are darkened by suggestions of menace; the home was a conflicted region for Beatrix.

At 2 Bolton Gardens, surrounded by what novelist Wilkie Collins described as 'the clean desolation, the neat ugliness, the prim torpor' of mid-Victorian urban development, Beatrix Potter was born on 28 July 1866.[11] The new streets rang with the calls of bakers' boys and, at times of particular concern, news-criers shouting headlines late into the evening. On horse-drawn buses, conductors blew brass horns 'to summon up the old gentlemen going to their city offices'; the hooves of carriage horses, including the Potters' own, sounded 'clump clop'.[12] In their wake, a crossing-sweeper plied his trade. Rats abounded, hunted by street urchins. Beatrix remembered watching their sport from the nursery window, 'a very favourite amusement' for its participants.[13] Especially in the autumn, fog hung heavy along the grey thoroughfares. For those prepared to look for them, last vestiges remained of a different past: the May Day celebration, near Kensington Square, of dancing round a 'Jack-in-the-green', a male figure covered in leaves. Beatrix described milkmaids flocking to the spectacle. As in eighteenth-century engravings, they wore 'straw hats, aprons, & ribbons'.[14] She would always take an interest in the details of historic dress.

Bolton Gardens was Beatrix Potter's home for more than half her life: she never regarded it with affection. 'My brother and I were born in London because my father was a lawyer there,' she told an American bookseller the year before she died, clutching after an explanation;[15] her heart roved elsewhere. Aged seventeen, she protested in her diary, 'Why do people live in London so much?' In the capital it was impossible to see the sky. Rows of houses, she claimed, shut her in like 'great frowning hills'. It was, simply, 'a horrid place'.[16] And 2 Bolton Gardens, despite the climbing rose that afterwards cloaked at least one wall, the fig tree in the garden, the neat rectangle of lawn framed by its path, perfect for sedate games with a succession of pets, and the drainpipes where robins and wrens fought for nest space,[17] was a behemoth of a house. 'A dark Victorian mausoleum,' one observer called it.[18] Despite appearances, Beatrix would remember her upbringing there as spartan.[19]

She was a pretty child (notwithstanding Millais's statement that her face was spoiled by an overlong nose and upper lip). Her elders approved her ready blushes and dressed her 'in print frock[s] and striped stockings'.[20] She sounds something like the North Country 'bonny lass', Bonny Arnot, of *The Fairy Caravan*, which Beatrix wrote in 1929: 'Blue were her eyes like the wood violet's blue, fair were her locks like the mary-bud's gold, and her red-and-white dimples like roses on snow!'[21] When she was three and still an only child (her brother Bertram, known as Bertie, was not born until March 1872), her father wrote to Millais about a portrait the painter had recently undertaken of nine-year-old Nina Lehmann, a businessman's daughter. 'When I look upon that picture,' he wrote wonderingly, despite the difference in the girls' ages, 'I am looking at my child.'[22]

Early photographs of Beatrix, taken by Rupert, make good the comparison. Millais's vision of Nina Lehmann is as much an archetype of contemporary prettiness as John Tenniel's Alice in his illustrations for *Alice's Adventures in Wonderland*, which Beatrix first saw the same year she received Rupert's duck sketches: limpid gaze, rosebud mouth, wavy flaxen hair (in Beatrix's case, held in place by a black or brown band – velvet- or ribbon-covered, depending on the occasion – painfully 'fastened with a bit of elastic, looped over a button behind the ear' and combined with 'absurdly uncomfortable [clothes]; white piqué starched frocks just like Tenniel's *Alice*... and cotton stockings striped round and round like a zebra's legs'.[23]) But while first photographs of Beatrix indicate lively and unmistakeable strength of will, Miss Lehmann – limply twirling a pink camellia, collared doves at her feet – is more demonstrably passive. Beatrix grew up to embody both impulses, as well as the contradiction this implies. Her relationship with her parents included a struggle between daughterly submission – endorsed by society and never fully rejected by Beatrix – and her determination, as she wrote in 1883, sooner or later to 'do something'.[24] Rupert Potter declined Millais's offer to paint Beatrix's portrait on the grounds that it might lead to vanity.

The Potters' world was one of conformities and prohibitions. Rupert Potter disguised aimlessness as urbanity; Helen Potter consumed infinite leisure in an unvarying social round of a sort Beatrix parodied in her descriptions of Tabitha Twitchit's tea parties. Holidays and extended visits punctuated identical years. The household at 2 Bolton Gardens apparently functioned with stultifying regularity. Insofar as their actions affected Beatrix, the indoor staff – George Cox the butler, Sarah Harper the cook and her sister, housekeeper Elizabeth – were clockwork puppets. Mr Cox excelled at polishing silver and folding napkins; Sarah Harper shortly escaped to marry a Scottish game-keeper met on a Potter family holiday. When Cox fell ill, appearances were kept up by 'a bandy-legged youth named William who answer[ed] to the name of Alfred'.[25]

For Beatrix in the nursery few things threatened the even tenor of repetitive days. Recent in origin – and further tainted by family traditions of religious dissent – her parents' wealth derived from trade: the grit, graft and canniness of enterprising North Country forebears. Thirty years earlier, Rupert's father, Edmund Potter, had established a calico printing works at Dinting Vale out-side Manchester; it became the largest of its sort in the world. The John Leech Company of cotton merchants, begun around the same time by Helen's father in nearby Stalybridge, had its own textile mills and shipping fleet. By 1866, neither imposed on its beneficiaries responsibility or excessive duties; Rupert and Helen Potter disdained to dwell on the source of their good fortune.

Rupert made good the vacuum with a fretful concern for his investments. Out of kilter with the reformist spirit of the times, his Liberal politics were decidedly conservative. Apprehensively he absorbed himself in current affairs. He had a horror of public unrest, 'such a terror of any disturbance or violence'; he regularly threatened emigration 'to the Colonies, Edinburgh, quiet provincial towns'.[26] His love of order extended to excessive punctuality over travel arrangements, days unnecessarily 'spent more or less on the railway [station]'.[27] He was assiduous in his attendance at his clubs (the Reform and the Athenaeum) and visiting galleries. In 1869 he was elected a member of the Photographic Society of London; critically, he read the newspapers, *The Field, Punch*. As a raconteur he seems to have possessed charm and humour, for all his forbidding appearance; Beatrix inherited his taste for risible anecdotes. Rupert, not Helen, was the lynchpin of this second generation of wealthy Northern dissenters. It was Rupert's friends – Liberal politician John Bright, educationalist and Unitarian minister William Gaskell (widower of the novelist Elizabeth) – who supplemented family and extended family in the Potters' social round.

Their background in trade, as well as their religious position outside the Church of England, excluded the Potters from much of London society. 'Intimate with all the rich and respectable Unitarians' families', they existed in a comfortable if unfashionable periphery.[28] One of eight children herself – including an alcoholic brother, William – Helen must have played some part in organising this interaction. She emerges from surviving sources as a two-dimensional character, with a taste for needlework, tea and the seaside, and 'disagreeable' in her dislikes.[29] She devoted her afternoons to paying calls. Her dinner party menus betray the elaborate excesses of the age: 'eight courses; not much of anything, but truly elegant', like those of Johnny Townmouse, and all served on Minton plates. More than once she received compliments on her resemblance to Queen Victoria; Beatrix described her as having very fat arms. There are suggestions of snobbery – like Amabella Tidler in *The Tale of the Faithful Dove*, who chooses to forget that her great-great-grandmother was an acrobat. At 2 Bolton Gardens, 'business' seldom intruded unbidden upon the lives of Beatrix's parents. Material comfort was the opiate.

At first Beatrix was never alone. Significantly, her earliest memory was not of London but a house in the country and birdsong – awakening as a baby in a crib, startled by the sound of birds in a hollow elm opposite the kitchen window at her grandparents' house in Hertfordshire. (The kitchen was full of flies, and in time Beatrix would discover that the hollow tree could be climbed from within to spy on owls and starlings.[30]) Jeopardising this idyll was her Scottish nurse, Ann McKenzie, who remained with the Potters until some time after Bertram was born. McKenzie's path to the nursery had been thorny. An elopement in her teens, followed by the death of her husband, had left her destitute with four children, all of whom she entrusted to the care of a family called Swift, while she struggled single-handed to earn a living in London. Beatrix's unflattering description of her as tyrannical and cross may well have been true.[31]

Beatrix's memory of her early childhood was unusually acute; an attachment to her memories – recollections 'as [clear] as the brightness of rich Scotch sunshine on... threadbare carpet'[32] – became an aspect of her make-up. 'I have been laughed at for what I say I can remember; but it is admitted that I can remember quite plainly from one and two years old,' she wrote later, with a hint of defiance.[33]

As in so many similar households, Beatrix's nursery was hermetic. Neither parent appears to have involved themselves unduly in third-floor life: their remoteness was shaped by convention, habit and, almost certainly, inclination. Unlike Tabitha Twitchit in *The Tale of Samuel Whiskers*, they were not then anxious parents (even considering Rupert's fidgetiness). They did not trouble themselves about friends for Beatrix. Other people's children threatened germs or, worse, bad influences, and Beatrix did not form acquaintances among the children of her parents' neighbours. She never would.

Instead Nurse McKenzie imparted first impressions and something more than a nurse's surveillance or solicitude. Her Calvinist bromides conveyed to her infant charge an unflinching assessment of human frailty. She sang hymns, read aloud from the Old Testament. 'The sweet rhythm of the authorised translation' made a lasting impression;[34] Beatrix remained a Bible reader into adulthood.[35] Sin played its part in what Beatrix termed Nurse McKenzie's 'terrible' creed. There was mention of witches and dark magic. Like the maid in a story called 'The Hobgoblin' by Maria Edgeworth, whose writing for children Beatrix read when young, she may have frightened her charge with 'a hundred foolish stories... particularly one about a black-faced goblin'.

On the nursery bookshelves, tales of stark didacticism reiterated the ugly warnings. Her least favourite – Sarah Trimmer's eighty-year-old *The Story of the Robins*, in which a human family and a family of robins unite in embracing virtue – Beatrix remembered as 'a fat stodgy book' and hated it roundly. In time a handful of what she called in 1912 her 'many books about well-behaved people' would include a moral, though without the aspect of hellfire and brimstone. In Beatrix's writing instruction emerged more playfully. Like Miss Louisa Pussycat in *The Fairy Caravan*, she enjoyed long words: 'soporific', 'volatile', 'the amelioration of disposition', 'lamentable want of discretion'. Her tales reflect Victorian parenting habits: discipline and punishments for all; rewards only for the well behaved. They punish 'frivolity' and 'impertinence', repeatedly through fear. And they delight in an elegant irony, which may be lost on younger readers.

Happily, Nurse McKenzie's role was not restricted to spiritual alarmism. The Potters were Unitarians, earnestly so in Rupert's case; Helen seems to have been less committed in her devotions. Unitarianism rejected the doctrine of the Trinity: it regarded Jesus as a human intermediary between man and God. Rationalism and a focus on conscience underpinned this dissenting faith; rationalism came to underpin Beatrix's beliefs. It was a habit of mind as much as a belief system. Pragmatic, it was capable of counterbalancing the grim assurances of Calvinism and, potentially, of responding to the century's spiritual challenges: notably, in the decade of Beatrix's birth, an ongoing debate on creationism provoked by Darwin's *On the Origin of Species*. The Unitarian services Beatrix attended with her parents once they considered her old enough must have tempered the vim of Ann McKenzie's sharp tenets. So, too, to her credit, the latter's choice of reading material for Beatrix. Books like *Uncle Tom's Cabin*, Harriet Beecher Stowe's story of 'a good, steady, sensible, pious fellow', and Charles Kingsley's *The Water Babies*, both read aloud by Nurse McKenzie, encouraged simple Christian goodness and compassion. Yet for an imaginative little girl alone in her third-floor nursery, neither 'improving' novels nor Calvinist strictures could rival in allure Nurse McKenzie's taste for fairy tales or her firm belief in fairies. Both would shape Beatrix's imaginative life in the long term.

Beatrix remembered looking for fairies as a child on holiday – making 'a fairyland for myself amongst the wild flowers, the animals, fungi, mosses, woods and streams, all the thousand objects of the countryside': a legacy of Ann McKenzie's storytelling.[36] Fairy tales thrilled her. She enjoyed *Undine*, the early-nineteenth-century German romance, read in an English translation: the story of a water sprite who marries a knight to gain a soul. Of it she remembered 'as a small child [making] illustrations for the works of Monsieur le Baron de la Motte Fouqué!... [The drawings] were very bad but the devil was so unpleasantly terrific, that it used to keep me awake at nights, though of my own manufacture.'[37] At her grandparents' house, exploring basement domestic offices on her own, she found a window that, inexplicably, would not open: 'I used to sit there for hours looking into the stableyard and wondering if there was an enchanted Prince below'.[38] Later she painted illustrations for scenes from 'Cinderella', 'Sleeping Beauty' and 'Tom Thumb'; she wrote her own version of 'Puss in Boots', *Kitty in Boots*, unsuccessfully offered to her publishers in 1914; in old age she conceived an unfulfilled wish 'to do a set of fairy tales in thin volumes'.[39] One story likens a tranquil seaside town to 'the Castle of Sleeping Beauty', while ten of her stories begin, like fairy tales, 'Once upon a time'.[40] *The Fairy Caravan* includes her own fairy story, 'The Fairy in the Oak'. She described herself as a child 'acquainted with fairies'.[41]

Looking for fairies formed a part of afternoon walks with her nurse in Kensington Gardens or the Gardens of the Royal Horticultural Society, then sited between Queen's Gate and Exhibition Road; or to the South Kensington Museum (today's Victoria and Albert Museum), opened in 1857 and in Beatrix's childhood resembling a large conservatory in its still leafy surrounds. All lay within easy distance of Bolton Gardens.

Nurse McKenzie's surprising belief suggests a streak of Highland whimsy in an otherwise unsentimental figure. Whatever her intention, that fancy provided Beatrix's initial encouragement to look beyond the appearance of things and glimpse the world imaginatively. Fairies and storytelling overlapped; fairies meant secrets, magic, another layer of fascination to the natural world. In time, fairy magic played its part in Beatrix's tales: in the crooked sixpence that, on Christmas Eve, found its way into a doll's stocking in *The Tale of Two Bad Mice*; in the miraculous workmanship of the Mayor of Gloucester's wedding clothes, completed while the feverish Tailor slept. Beatrix the author simply recast fairies as mice.

At Rupert Potter's insistence, Christmas Day in Bolton Gardens was treated as an ordinary Sunday, without the excesses or the enchantment of that favourite childhood festival; Beatrix remembered it as less cheerful than other people's Christmases. A surviving present she gave to her mother – a small beechwood box, bought for 6¾d, with her own decoupage decoration of painted mice – certainly appears a modest gift. Even as an adult, still living with her parents, Beatrix envied neighbours' Christmas trees 'with the little doll angel up on the top'.[42] An early attempt at financial independence – producing commercial designs for Christmas cards in her twenties – also represented independence of spirit. Little wonder that, in such a climate, she formed the habit as a child of seeking out the remarkable in the everyday. Drawing provided her earliest passport; so, too, looking at pictures, 'which seemed almost alive'.[43] First her parents encouraged her drawing. Afterwards her governess, Miss Hammond, added her voice and, later still,

Beatrix undertook courses in watercolour and oil painting with specialist tutors.

In a small homemade sketchbook, begun in the spring of 1876, when she was nine years old, Beatrix drew and coloured sketches of rabbits. Like Rupert's bonneted duck, most wore clothes. They wore spectacles, struggled with an inside-out umbrella, skimmed over ice or snow on sleds and sleighs. A lively squirrel accompanied them, running like Beatrix's cairn terrier, Sandy. The rabbits walked on two legs, as would the animals of Beatrix's fiction.

At this stage they did not overwhelm her output, which also encompassed landscapes and nature studies, including unusually assured pencil drawings of flowers: narcissus, foxglove and periwinkle. The flowers may have been copied from primers or drawing manuals, like Vere Foster's Drawing-Copy Books, published in the 1860s, though Millais himself commended young Beatrix's powers of observation. Less in evidence were London sights. The capital scarcely touched Beatrix's art. In time she would exclude it from her fiction. Even in her late teens, her experience of London was mostly confined to the vicinity of Bolton Gardens.

A matter-of-fact little person, was the grown-up Beatrix's verdict on her childhood self, looking back after an interval of half a century.[44] She grew up to value common sense.

Her older self underestimated the extent of her childish imagination: she was fanciful and romantic, sometimes to the point of feyness. She was robust in her attitude to nature, as she would remain, with an unsqueamish curiosity about natural phenomena. Her interest in fairies was something different, a childhood whim and, at the same time, a nostalgic impulse of a sort that never left her; throughout her life she believed in the existence of the Loch Ness monster.[45] Her interior life then was not especially remarkable, and her pencil, like her mind, ranged widely. She was a serious child and, in her own assessment, old-fashioned.[46] Her head would be turned – but not by Bolton Gardens or the careful, conventional world of her parents.

· 2 ·

'I do wish we lived in the country'

Rupert Potter's many photographs of his only daughter capture her elfin prettiness. 'Blue were her eyes like the wood violet's blue, fair were her locks like the marybud's gold,' Beatrix later wrote of a 'bonny lass', a fitting description of herself when young.

'Birds' Place that I remember was in Hertfordshire,
long ago when I was young. Perhaps the elms
and chestnuts have been felled; the passing
swallows say the cedar is blown down.'

The Fairy Caravan, 1929

THE CHINA that made its way, several times daily, to
the third-floor nursery – bearing plain-cooked meat,
simple puddings or bread to be eaten with milk – included
plates decorated in blue on a white ground, with pictures
of birds and animals. Today several hang in Beatrix Potter's
Lake District farmhouse, Hill Top. Again the drawings were
Rupert's, the china specially made for Bolton Gardens to
his own design. Impossible that Beatrix should remember
a time when her attention was not drawn to and by the
natural world, or when nature did not appear uppermost
among subjects for her pencil and paintbox.

Determined respectability and a degree of social isolation notwithstanding, 2 Bolton Gardens offered Beatrix
spurs to imagination. Rupert Potter and Helen Leech had
sketched in their youth; Beatrix grew familiar with the

sight of her parents busy with their sketchbooks on visits to the country or coast. Before her marriage Helen Leech painted landscapes in watercolour: accomplished, lady-like exercises that betray little of the hand behind them. Although Rupert did not paint, the directness and sure touch of his drawing appealed to Beatrix. If her mother approached art as a tool in her social armoury or diversion for leisurely days, her father's engagement was more vigorous. Rupert had inherited his taste for art from his own father, one-time president of the Manchester School of Art and, in 1857, among organisers of *The Art Treasures of Great Britain* exhibition of 16,000 works of art, held on a three-acre site in Old Trafford. Rupert Potter was a regular visitor to the Royal Academy; he visited commercial galleries and London auction houses. As a teenager Beatrix accompanied him – as she accompanied him on his calls to Millais at 2 Palace Gate, a building of ersatz aristocratic splendour utterly remote from the houses Beatrix chose for herself when she too achieved commercial success. Rupert's youngest sister Lucy shared his enthusiasm for photography and won a clutch of medals from the Photographic Society of London; beginning in 1873, Rupert showed photographs of his own in the society's exhibitions. Both John Leech and Edmund Potter had assembled collections of paintings. Among the former's acquisitions was a landscape by Turner, which Beatrix saw in Grandmother Leech's London house in Palace Gardens, while Edmund's purchase of works by Landseer, Etty, Millais, Leighton and animalier Briton Rivière suggests an active interest in the art of his time; in addition, he collected Chinese enamels and porcelain.[1] Among Helen's sisters-in-law was Rosalie Ansdell, daughter of animal painter and Royal Academician Richard Ansdell.[2] Art formed a connective thread in the lives of Potter and Leech relations; it was an occupation – and a preoccupation – for both sexes, and a subject for conversation within the family circle. Throughout her childhood an interest in art, even at its simplest level, drew Beatrix closer to her father. Rupert called Beatrix 'B'. During his absences from Bolton Gardens he wrote her letters about animals, gardens or the progress of her frequent colds.

As we have seen, it was Rupert who provided Beatrix with material for copying in the form of his own sketches, and Rupert who, intentionally or otherwise, first encouraged Beatrix to look beyond typically 'feminine' subjects in her drawing. In 1859, in *Women Artists in All Ages and Countries*, historian Elizabeth Ellet had explained that female artists were particularly suited to flower and still-life paintings, since 'such occupations might be pursued in the strict seclusion of home, to which custom and public sentiment assigns the fair student', a conventional statement of its time. Although Beatrix made many early flower drawings, her horizons were broader, inspired not only by personal inclination but Rupert's sketches, the nursery china, birds in the garden, wildlife glimpsed on visits to the country.

Beatrix's tenth birthday present, 'bound in scarlet with a gilt edge', was a copy of *Birds Drawn from Nature*, by Mrs Hugh Blackburn.[3] Beatrix devoured its plates with the relish of a connoisseur, washing her hands before she allowed herself to touch the hallowed pages. She particularly admired the pictures of 'the young Herring Gull and the Hoody Crow'. She described the book, bought for her by her parents, as a gift from her father. For Beatrix, animals, picture books and drawing were Rupert's enthusiasms more than Helen's, though her diary records at least one instance of mother and daughter visiting an exhibition together without Rupert.[4]

Her childhood coincided with developments in children's publishing, including a sophisticated process of colour wood-block printing of illustrations called chromoxylography. Companies like Dean & Son and Raphael Tuck & Sons produced so-called 'movable' books, with pop-up, fold-down or cut-out details: pictures 'moved' to mirror events described in the story. Dean's three-dimensional 'Scenic Books' were first published in 1856, in a series that included *Little Red Riding Hood, Cinderella,*

Robinson Crusoe and *Aladdin*.[5] In the 1870s artists Walter Crane, Kate Greenaway and Randolph Caldecott began illustrating and decorating a range of books for children, including, in Crane's case, the popular children's novels of Mrs Molesworth, which Beatrix read as they were published, and *The Baby's Opera*. Clearly Crane's illustrations appealed to Beatrix. (By contrast she remembered 'ungratefully getting rid of a Kate Greenaway birthday book': 'compared with Caldecott,' she noted, 'she could not draw'.[6]) Her copy of a picture of 'Mrs Bond' from *The Baby's Opera*, an innocent-looking depiction of a woman on the brink of killing and stuffing with sage the ducklings in her pond, survives in a sketchbook from 1877.[7] In format, such books gave equal prominence to design and written content. Three decades later, the same balance would characterise Beatrix's own books, with the further innovation that in Beatrix's books text and illustrations were fully integrated.

Since Rupert Potter's nursery forays were limited, and Helen Potter seems to have struggled to put her daughter at her ease, it was as well Beatrix enjoyed the books in the nursery bookcase and Nurse McKenzie's stories. By way of alternative she claimed to care for two toys only: 'a dilapidated black wooden doll called Topsy' and a flannelette pig of grubby appearance that remained mostly out of reach in a drawer in her grandparents' library.[8] Perhaps surprisingly, she discounted the small toy rabbit with which Rupert photographed her, in company with her cousin Alice Crompton Potter, when she was five. Unlike the owner of the doll's house in *The Tale of Two Bad Mice*, she was not especially attached to her three toys.

Until the age of six she spent long intervals alone with her nurse, plagued by headaches and colds. On rainy days there were no walks with Nurse McKenzie to Kensington Gardens; catching a cold led to prohibitions against going outside at all. In the nursery, a fire lit against the chill, she listened to stories read aloud. Later she read to herself. She also learned passages by heart.

When she was about seven, Beatrix accomplished a remarkable feat in committing to memory all six cantos of Walter Scott's romantic narrative poem, *The Lady of the Lake*. Scott's historical tale is boldly coloured. It delights, in passing, in the flora of its West Highlands setting – eglantine, hawthorn, hazel, 'primrose pale', violet, foxglove and nightshade – conjuring up a rich natural cornucopia of a sort Beatrix would celebrate in many paintings as well as passages of *The Fairy Caravan*. Years later, troubled by sleeplessness in her twenties, she learnt by heart entire plays by Shakespeare: *The Tempest, The Merchant of Venice, A Midsummer Night's Dream* and a clutch of history plays; in her journal she plotted the extent of her mastery.

Aside from mental stamina, both undertakings point to the empty hours at her disposal. Like Griselda, the heroine of Mrs Molesworth's *The Cuckoo Clock*, published when she was eleven, the young Beatrix might have reflected of her sequestered existence, 'It was very dull. It got duller and duller.' Unlike Griselda, she occupied the yawning days; she was not 'obliged to spend the time in sleeping, for want of anything better to do'.[9] She was an imaginative, spirited, evidently diligent child and, in her own assess-ment, 'a cheerful person'; she read and, as if obsessively, she drew.[10] Her childhood memories do not indicate un-happiness. Until Bertram was old enough to become a companion, and afterwards when he went away to school, Beatrix – a girl denied friends – entertained herself. Self-containment was an important facet of her make-up. It surfaces in her fictional characters: Jeremy Fisher, Mrs Tiggy-winkle, Mrs Tittlemouse. All live apparently fulfilled, largely solitary lives.

She loved riddles, rhymes and nonsense poems; the taste stayed with her and influenced her own written style. As late as March 1900, aged twenty-three, she 'went to the Reading Room at the British Museum... to see a delightful old book full of rhymes' and was thrilled by her morning's occupation.[11] Riddles and rhymes play their part in *The Tale of Squirrel Nutkin* and the original, longer, privately printed version of *The Tailor of Gloucester*; *The Tale of Little Pig Robinson*, first begun in 1883, offers a coda of sorts to Edward Lear's 'The Owl and the Pussycat', which Beatrix encountered as a child. In several tales, notably *The Sly Old Cat*, the boundary separating rhyme and prose is fluid. Elsewhere, Beatrix employed two-part sentences, broken by a semicolon. Psalm-like in rhythm and cadence, their effect is both humorous and sonorous.[12] She insisted she 'several times used piled up adjectives', which further shapes the particular tip-tilt of her prose.[13]

So wholehearted was Beatrix's absorption, aged seven, in *The Lady of the Lake* that she remembered 'crying bitterly because Ellen Douglas was an R.C. [Roman Catholic] and therefore must have gone to hell'.[14] Alone in her nursery, like many imaginative children Beatrix experienced fiction as an alternative reality; she retained the imprint of her early exposure to stories and poems.

Her parents concerned themselves with her amusement intermittently. She learnt needlework and knitting; later she painted designs for embroidered borders for cloths and herself embroidered a cotton brocade pelmet for her four-poster bed.[15] We do not know if it was Helen Potter, Ann McKenzie or her governess Miss Hammond who taught her. Before her marriage, Helen had played her part in Stalybridge philanthropy, encouraged by her own mother:

she taught millworkers' daughters needlework and cookery. In London she transcribed books into braille for a blindness charity. Beatrix knitted as a child and included her knitting among her holiday packing; she learned to darn too. Neither became a consuming pastime.

Shortly before she died, Beatrix dismissed her choice of childhood reading matter as 'silly stories about other little girls' doings' and 'trash... goody-goody, powder-in-the-jam books'.[16] It was only partly true. Beatrix taught herself to read on Walter Scott's 'Waverley' novels, influenced by her enjoyment of *The Lady of the Lake*, the bookshelves at Bolton Gardens and Nurse McKenzie's storytelling. Tales of stirring derring-do, with a marked sense of place and the lilt of local voices, Scott's novels had reinvented the past for Beatrix's grandparents' generation. Her own writing came to share the 'Waverley' novels' regional tang, rooted in a particular landscape. It, too, exploited distinctive speech patterns, although the dialogue of Beatrix's twenty-one tales was more strongly influenced by her reading, especially her enjoyment of Jane Austen, than any local dialect. In *The Fairy Caravan* and North Country stories like 'Pace Eggers' she celebrated her later conviction that 'no tongue can be as musical as Lancashire'.[17]

Beatrix traced the breakthrough in her reading to her second attempt at *Rob Roy*. She admitted to missing out the long words. Her enjoyment was unimpaired and she went on to read Scott's novels 'over and over'; unsurprisingly she conceived a passionate desire to visit Edinburgh.[18] As a child she could not have anticipated how nearly in outline *Rob Roy* would resemble the story of her own life. Scott's hero, Frank Osbaldistone, is the child of a wealthy Londoner. He is banished to the north of England, but afterwards rewarded with the gift of the family home, Osbaldistone Hall. Beatrix, too, would turn her back on London's comforts. In her case, her 'banishment' to the Lake District was voluntary, akin to a self-imposed exile, but no less a breach with the world she had known. As she saw it, like Osbaldistone's it represented a return to ancestral acres.

Subsequently Beatrix regarded the house in Bolton Gardens without affection: she excluded it from any summary of formative influences; at the end of her life she did not lament its destruction in the Blitz. Yet it was there, through protracted years in the nursery, beginning as a small child, that she learned to view the world as a reader, an important step on her journey towards re-envisioning the world as a writer. In its layout – separate spaces for parents, children and servants – Bolton Gardens asserted the hierarchies of Victorian family life: a critique of social convention is a source of humour in a handful of Beatrix's tales, including *The Tale of the Pie and the Patty-Pan* and

The Tale of Tom Kitten. For the young Beatrix, confinement on the third floor involved a measure of loneliness. Books, stories, drawing and painting barricaded her against the gulf. It was in Bolton Gardens that Beatrix viewed possibilities of life beyond those orderly purlieus, possibilities made real to her from infancy by the Potter habits of reading, sketching... and travel.

'When I was a child I used to go to the seaside for holidays,' Beatrix Potter wrote in *The Tale of Little Pig Robinson*, which she set in the fictional town of Stymouth (an amalgam of Sidmouth, Teignmouth, Lyme Regis and Hastings). Those holidays mostly took place in April, when 2 Bolton Gardens was spring-cleaned, redecorated or newly carpeted and, like the unnamed family in *The Tale of Johnny Town-Mouse*, Rupert, Helen, Beatrix and Bertram Potter repaired to a south coast watering place and hotels that frequently fell short of their exacting standards. (The 'excellent' but costly Imperial Burdon Hotel in Weymouth, for example, disappointed in April 1895 as there were 'fan-lights over the doors which makes it awkward to change photographic slides'.[19])

For long weeks at the end of every summer, beginning when Beatrix was four, the Potters also stayed in the Highlands, continuing a tradition started by Edmund Potter: holidays of fishing, stalking and, for Beatrix and, in turn, Bertram, the chance of temporary misrule. For eleven years, from 1871, Rupert rented a severe-looking house on the banks of the River Tay in Perthshire: Dalguise House, with many windows and dense shrubberies. There, friends joined the family party: Millais, Gaskell and Bright; so, too, Potter and Leech relations. The men enjoyed first-rate sport. Rupert photographed their catch: salmon laid out on the lawn like bloated offerings. He photographed Helen, Beatrix and Bertram, and Beatrix with her governess. He photographed dogs and, repeatedly, the same elegant stone column in the Dalguise garden, twined about with climbing roses and crowned with a unicorn. He set the camera so that he, too, could take his place alongside fish or statuary, heavily whiskered and invariably frowning.

Beatrix and Bertram roamed through gardens 'laden with the smell of roses', noisy with bees and the whine of bluebottle flies, through expanses of heather, through 'the dark glades of Craig Donald Wood', where wind murmured in the fir trees and, on grey days, thunder growled thrillingly in the distance.[20] The siblings caught rabbits, listened out for roe deer and the evening cry of the nightjar, collected birds' eggs, animal skeletons and plums from an ancient tree; Beatrix picked flowers for drawing or pressing; 'in the hollow between the two sleepers in the goods siding at Dalguise, where trucks were constantly shunted over the bird's head', she found a partridge nest 'with an incredible number of eggs'.[21] Brother and sister revelled in a natural paradise, as companionable as Timmy and Goody Tiptoes in the nut thicket in *The Tale of Timmy Tiptoes*. In a homemade sketchbook, Beatrix drew and painted the Dalguise grounds and surrounding sights, including 'the Duchess of Athole's [*sic*] model dairy'.[22] In her memory she stowed away the images that would recall to her 'that peaceful past time of childhood' and buttress her against unhappiness later, her memories a shield and a screen.[23] She stockpiled memories in the same way Mrs Tittlemouse hoards cherry stones and thistle-down seed. And often her memories were visual, snapshots like photographs: 'a white cat basking in the sunset at a barn door high up in the wall';[24] 'a rambling old house full of aviaries and pets, doves cooing, and beautiful Persian cats walking about under the rookery on the lawn'.[25]

In the Highlands, Beatrix found herself 'half believing' Nurse McKenzie's fairy stories and folk tales; she would remember 'seeing my own fancies so clearly [there] that they became true to me'.[26] She devised stories, she painted, including, in 1878, a picture of trees, 'The Three Witches of Birnam Woods'.[27] Scotland was a catalyst: her Scottish holidays allowed Beatrix to substantiate imaginative flights of fancy. Although she set most of her books in the Lake District, it was in Perthshire that such stories, with their necessary suspension of disbelief, acquired an aspect of possibility. There she 'live[d] in fairyland'.[28] Helen Potter took with her to Scotland her London servants and her carriage – coachman and groom in white breeches and top boots, their coats with brass buttons showing the Potter family crest: the festal mood could be tempered by sameness. On later holidays there would be a pony and phaeton for Beatrix.

With holidays at the seaside and in Scotland and trips to stay with relatives, the Potters spent up to four months of the year absent from Bolton Gardens. Family visits took them over the old wooden bridge to Putney – where at Putney Park, within easy reach of central London, an elderly cousin kept cattle, ducks and 'a splendid breed of black Berkshire pigs'; she had planted her garden with cabbage roses.[29] Until 1884, they travelled north to Stalybridge. There, at Grandmother Leech's house, Gorse Hall, even the doormat impressed itself on Beatrix's memory; as a small child, the bedroom passage 'seem[ed] dark and mysterious', shadowed by 'the terror that flieth by night'.[30] As she grew older, Beatrix would visit Helen's sister, Harriet, who had married another cotton magnate, Fred Burton, and settled in Denbighshire; she stayed with relatives of Rupert's mother 'on the edge of the Cotswolds, overlooking the vale of Severn'.[31] Best of all, until the house was sold in 1891, were frequent sorties to the home of her Potter grandparents in Hertfordshire.

Edmund Potter's remarkable career had taken him from calico printing to Parliament, where he sat as Liberal MP for Carlisle. In the way of the newly rich, he bought a house in London and a country house at a comfortable remove from the source of his wealth. Camfield Place, near Essendon in Hertfordshire, was 'a good-sized small-roomed old house of no particular pretensions, the outside, red brick, white-washed'[32] when Edmund Potter bought it, with 300 acres, from Lord Dimsdale in 1866. With typical Victorian confidence, he set about demolishing half the original house. He replaced it with 'a large addition curiously joined to the old part with steps and stairs... six sitting rooms and a porch below, six bedrooms and two dressing rooms above, with a good deal of wasted space under the gables', the whole glaringly faced with yellow brick.[33]

It was a commonplace structure, the principal rooms, as Beatrix admitted, too large for comfort, the terrace on the north front windy, the most important, oak-panelled room of the old house destroyed in her grandfather's remodelling. Nevertheless, glimpsed through the eyes of childhood it was 'a palatial residence'.[34] The room that engaged Beatrix longest, when she recorded her memories of Camfield, predated Potter ownership. A 'little old room' and 'spotless', it was lined with painted panelling and cupboards, with a whitewashed ceiling, pretty wallpaper and a view over flowerbeds.[35] It sounds like rooms she made for herself much later at Hill Top and used in her stories of Tom Kitten and Samuel Whiskers; a room like Ribby's kitchen in *The Tale of the Pie and the Patty-Pan* or, like Mrs Tiggy-winkle's, spick and span and cosy. She discovered this neat little service room as a child, wandering alone through passages and pantries. Its very distinctness from Bolton Gardens caught her imagination.

Happily Edmund Potter's 'improvements' to Camfield Place concentrated on the house. Aside from some over-zealous planting of shrubs, and more successful horse chestnut plantings, he let the gardens alone – the work of Capability Brown, designed at the turn of the century. Brown's velvety undulations of greensward softened the assertive bulk of Edmund's new building: lawns spotted with trees, including 'two great cedars', their branches like 'outstretched arms', their green bark splashed with red, with 'orange butterflies flitt[ing], and red-tailed velvety bees'.[36] Fifteen gardeners tended the tranquil spaces. In Beatrix's childhood, Capability Brown's vision, combined with Edmund Potter's deep pockets, sculpted a landscape of artificial loveliness maintained in an equally artificial state of near perfection – as sleek and pristine as Mrs Blackburn's specimens of painted bird life or the flowers in Beatrix's primers. And so Beatrix's first experiences of country life – memories that stretched back even to her crib – contained significant elements of sham: a manmade idyll sustained by the spoils of invisible industry. It was at Camfield that she absorbed what she described as 'a pictorial sense of trees arranged in landscape'.[37] Decades later, the same sense would influence her efforts as a conservationist. It was based on a picturesque illusion.

She would not be able to remember a time that she had not known and loved Camfield. It was her childish ideal of perfection and, afterwards, cherished as 'the place I love best in the world'.[38] It perfectly fitted a vision of the country belonging to the child of wealthy London parents, and Beatrix relished everything about it that spoke to her of distance from her third-floor life in Kensington: new-laid eggs; fresh milk in unlimited supply; Mrs Spriggins's loaves, their crusts dusted with flour; even the earthenware plates and lopsided candles in simple metal dishes used in the day and night nurseries. Beyond the wide lattice windows, visit after visit, the same tame robin occupied the same spot on a wall covered in yellow roses. Here the air was clean, free of London's sooty tinct. Bats flew at night, weasels skirmished in the hedgerows. In late spring pink candles spiked Edmund's new horse chestnuts; on summer mornings cuckoos called at daybreak. Beatrix recorded the autumn flight of wild ducks and wild geese. The stable clock tolled passing hours.

In the library, under a table, hidden by a cloth with yellow-green fringes, Beatrix played with the flannel-ette pig. Unseen, she listened to grown-up conversation, enthralled by her grandmother's reminiscences. She consumed gossip and family history alongside 'very hard gingersnap biscuits', which Jessy Potter dispensed from a canister.[39] On one occasion, she lost a tooth in the process. When she was older she explored the library bookshelves. At seventeen she was 'very much impressed' by editions of *The Iliad* and *The Odyssey* illustrated by neoclassicist John Flaxman. Devoured in happy hours at Camfield, Flaxman's drawings – characterised by clarity and precise outlines – became another influence on Beatrix's own work. She considered him 'the greatest English draughtsman that has ever lived'.[40]

At Camfield a tangible sense of plenty – in the distant farmyard as well as on the tea table – reassured Beatrix. In her response to her grandparents' estate, she was discernibly her parents' daughter. She applauded 'the feeling of... well-assured, indolent wealth, honourably earned and wisely spent, charity without ostentation, opulence without pride'.[41] With its subtext of just deserts and lack of swank, it was an attitude influenced by Unitarianism, which emphasised social responsibility and social conscience, and perhaps by the complacency of the newly rich. Whatever Rupert and Helen's social pretensions, their mindset lacked profligacy or fecklessness, failings of an indolent aristocracy.

A sense of honourable earnings and wise spending surfaces in Beatrix's story of the Flopsy Bunnies. 'Very improvident and cheerful', Benjamin Bunny and his wife Flopsy are not always able to provide 'quite enough to eat' for their large family, with results that threaten to go badly for the Flopsy Bunnies. The author's attitude to improvidence is mixed. Beatrix had a healthy regard for money and its sensible disposal. On a visit to Wales she referred to the 'lavish prodigality' by which a landowning family was 'reduced to living in the kitchen': her tone is amused but scornful.[42] And she had a taste for a bargain. She considered 'it greatly detracts from the enjoyment of a purchase if you have paid an exorbitant price', an echo of the shrewdness innate to both her grandfathers.[43] Her views on credit are clear to readers of *The Tale of Ginger and Pickles*. Her eventual decision to write children's stories about animals

OVER THE HILLS AND FAR AWAY

ought not to encourage us to consider her sentimental. Her family's recent history of entrepreneurialism left its imprint on this impressionable Victorian daughter.

Above all, Camfield's chief recommendation was its chatelaine, Jessy Potter. 'There is no one like grand-mamma,' Beatrix wrote: she thought her 'as near perfect as is possible'[44] and their bond partly filled the void caused by Beatrix's lack of intimacy with her mother. Jessy Potter was a yardstick against which Beatrix measured Helen Potter and found her wanting, a spirited old woman with a keen appreciation of her own charms, a taste for fast carriage driving and what seems like a well-honed ability to intimi-date at will.[45] She had a vigorous sense of family pride and the older generation's habit of expansive discourse on her antecedents. She imbued Beatrix with a lifelong fascination for her own family, the Cromptons, and a conviction that Crompton characteristics, as enlarged by her grandmother, should surface in her own nature; that Beatrix would later describe herself as a 'believer in breed' – heredity in all its forms – was Jessy's doing. As outlined by 'Grandmamma', the Cromptons were mavericks: as keen as mustard in their Unitarianism and politically rebellious, with rumours of a romantic attachment to Jacobitism; they were financially astute, appealingly pig-headed and, up to a point, self-regarding – tenacious, obstinate and indomitable, according to Beatrix.[46] In Grandmamma's version, Beatrix inherited a legacy of enterprise, bloody-mindedness, philanthropy and pluck. Unsurprisingly, the young Beatrix longed to align herself within that vigorous continuum. Implicit in her choice was a rejection of her parents' conventional compromises. In middle age, it was her Crompton forebears, not the Potters, who inspired Beatrix's admiration. 'I was very much attached to my grandmother Jessy Crompton and said to be very like her, "only not so good looking!!",' she wrote.[47]

Among details of her grandmother's childhood that found a later parallel in Beatrix's life was the purchase by Jessy's father, Abraham Crompton, of a Lake District farmhouse for summer holidays: Holme Ground, near Coniston. Years later, Beatrix was able to locate it from Hill Top, dimly visible on a distant horizon. Eventually she bought the farm herself.

When Beatrix was six, Nurse McKenzie left, to be replaced by a governess, Florrie Hammond, and the nursery took on the aspect of a schoolroom. In later life, Beatrix claimed that her education had been neglected: not unusually for the time, neither Rupert nor Helen appears seriously to have considered sending their daughter to school. (Helen was sceptical about public schools generally and, save Rupert's enthusiasm, would not have sent Bertram to Charterhouse.[48]) The assiduousness with which the Potters restricted Beatrix's social contact through her childhood and beyond makes their decision doubly unsurprising.

Beginning with Miss Hammond, Beatrix learnt English, maths, French, history and geography; in time there would be lessons in Latin and German. Her enjoyment proved uncertain. 'The rules of geography and grammar are tiresome,' she noted; 'there is no general word to express the feelings I have always entertained towards arithmetic.' 'I cannot do the simplest sum right,' she insisted.[49] With a degree of disingenuousness she subsequently claimed to have forgotten every historical date 'except William the Conqueror 1066', but she took pleasure in her reading of Virgil.[50] Her spelling and punctuation would remain idiosyncratic.

Miss Hammond understood her charge. Her regime made generous provision for drawing and painting and, in the winter of 1878, she recommended to the Potters that Beatrix receive drawing lessons from a specialist teacher. A Miss Cameron was engaged for 'freehand, model, geometry, perspective and a little water-colour flower painting', an arrangement that continued until May 1883.[51] Although her relationship with Beatrix deteriorated over time, Miss Cameron's encouragement, added to Rupert's, helped guide

Beatrix towards subjects for her art. Ditto the inspiration Beatrix drew from her reading, from the delightful mock arcadia of Camfield and the blandishments of Dalguise in its untamed Highland setting.

Art was a compulsion for Beatrix. 'I cannot rest, I must draw, however poor the result,' she wrote in her journal in October 1884.[52] Once, lacking any more absorbing subject (and to her own amusement), she drew the swill bucket. She drew Bertram, rams' heads, horses eating from nosebags; she drew cats and kittens, and mice dancing; she drew ivy clinging to a wall; she drew the paddle steamer moored at Holyhead. In a cottage in Kent she drew a pewter tankard and the wooden armchair she copied in her illustration to the rhyme 'How do you do, Mistress Pussy?', later included in *Cecily Parsley's Nursery Rhymes*; the Tailor of Gloucester sits in front of the fire in the same chair. Her painted sketches included fragments unearthed by excavations – remains of ancient shoes and sandals; images of three- and ten-spined sticklebacks presented side on and from above; the fossil of a giant water scorpion. In a study of 1896, she included on the same sheet of drawings images of rabbits, a caterpillar and a moth, an insect's leg greatly magnified, fungi in cross section and an earthenware pitcher.

Despite Miss Cameron's lessons, and subsequent un-happy lessons in oil painting with an unidentified Mrs A.,

Beatrix largely taught herself; she pursued her own inclinations. The question of specialising did not arise, for her interests were always clear and her need to paint unflagging. She would pursue her artist's vocation in tandem with her absorption in natural history to earn for herself, unintentionally, her singular place in history.

· 3 ·

'The irresistible desire to copy
any beautiful object which
strikes the eye'

Beatrix and her brother Bertram. Despite a six-year age gap, the siblings were devoted to one another, united by their fascination for animals and art.

'I am very well acquainted with
dear Mrs Tiggy-winkle!'

The Tale of Mrs Tiggy-Winkle, 1905

BEATRIX WAS FIFTEEN when she recorded her disappointment at the paintings included in the Summer Exhibition of the Royal Academy. Her chief complaint concerned absence of truth to nature: seagulls that looked 'uncommonly like ducks', 'very queer' carnations and 'rather queer' holly, 'very small and terribly spotty' leopards, 'a slightly deformed pug'.[1]

She knew what she was talking about. In 1875, at the age of eight, Beatrix had made a series of notes about moths, butterflies and birds' eggs. The caterpillar of the tiger moth, she wrote, 'feeds on the nettle and hawthorn and is found in June they are covered with black, white and red. They are found by road sides and lanes'. Of the drinker moth, she noted, 'I don't know what it eats, but I think it is the flowering nettle.'[2]

From the first awakening of interest nature was a serious

pursuit for Beatrix, based on detailed study: drawing, anno-
tation, record keeping. Following an afternoon's fishing the
summer of her seventeenth birthday, she filled half a diary
entry with a description of the respiratory habits of newts:
'The moment they have parted with the old [air] they
breathe rapidly through the nostrils like other reptiles, as
may be seen by the rapid palpitation of the throat; but... the
newt having put out the used-up air, draws in fresh by
quick respirations through its nostril.'[3] Methodically she
plotted the stages of the process; she contrasted it with
that of 'frogs and toads and salamanders'. Her observations
led her to a question about frogs: 'how can frogs stop under
water so long as they sometimes do, over half an hour?'[4] In
this instance, her naturalist's curiosity existed independent
of any desire to paint the newts that she and Bertram had
caught together. She was startled by their size and the noise
they made: an unexpected squeak. She noted the apparent
incongruity that 'the British smooth newt does, very rarely,
utter an extremely sweet whistling note'.[5] Another summer
she did undertake a painted study of a male newt, complete
with ruffled crest in the mating season. Its belly is carmine-
flushed, its body vividly spotted.

'I did so many careful botanical studies in my youth,'
Beatrix remembered in 1921. She prided herself that her
approach had been 'painstaking' and 'thorough'.[6] Her tally

was indeed considerable: she referred to her 'thousands' of sketches.[7] As a child she supplemented live plant specimens with illustrations copied from primers and, after 1882, John E. Sowerby's *British Wild Flowers*, a present from her grandmother. She enjoyed making lists, as if thoroughness were both an aim and an end in itself, like the catalogue of local bird life she itemised on a visit to Hertfordshire in 1883 (the same visit in which she encountered a family called 'Titmouse'[8]) and the record of garden birds – including absences – she kept at home in London.[9] And one interest led to another. 'The spirit of enquiry,' she offered sententiously, 'leads up a lane which hath no ending.'[10]

From lichens she proceeded to geology and fossils. On seaside holidays she collected shells and seaweed; she trained her opera glasses on seagulls, made forays with Bertram to discover the first primroses, watched fishermen catching crabs in basket cages and, off the coast of Tenby, puffins on an island. She explored quarries, nervous of the quarrymen, and taught herself how to use a cold chisel on the rocks she found there; on other occasions she came away empty-handed, as at Thief Fold Quarry in the Lake District, in August 1895, when a tip-off about trilobites proved unfounded.[11] Back in London, she walked the short distance to the Natural History Museum, visible from the nursery windows; there, 'working very industriously', she made careful drawings of geological specimens.[12] She glutted herself on fossils: 'I intend to pick up everything I find which is not too heavy.'[13] From the outset her nature study was marked by obsessiveness and resolve, and an unquenchable thirst; an elderly cousin called her 'the busy Bee'.[14] For respite there were afternoons with Bertram sailing his model boat in Kensington Gardens, or board games at home, including a game called 'Go-bang'.[15] On warm days she was allowed the use of a dressing room as a makeshift studio for her painting. Permission rested with her mother.

Thanks to Rupert's connection with Millais, Beatrix Potter's 'painstaking', 'thorough' and 'industrious' apprenticeship as an artist was served in the shadow of Pre-Raphaelitism. Millais's painting featured among conversational topics in Bolton Gardens. There were meetings with Millais and privileged access to view his latest pictures. Although he alarmed her and she does not appear to have admitted to him her determination to become an artist, Millais talked to Beatrix in a general way about the progress of her drawing or mixing colours. By the time Beatrix was old enough to consider his work dispassionately – taking issue on occasion with both his draughtsmanship and his colouring – Millais had foresworn the radicalism of his early, Pre-Raphaelite manner in favour of something more lucrative: sentimental potboilers and enamelled portraits of plutocrats (the latter in particular provoked Beatrix's disdain).

But Beatrix was wholehearted in her admiration for his early paintings. Their impact on her was powerful and lasting. 'I remember what a great impression those pictures made on me,' she wrote about *Isabella* and *Mariana*, which she first saw when she was fourteen; 'they were the first that ever struck me.'[16] She particularly admired Millais's outdoor Shakespearean subjects, *Ferdinand and Ariel* and *Ophelia*. She described the latter as 'one of the most marvellous pictures in the world'.[17] The precise natural details in both works – the trees and shrubs and flowers of the riverbanks, even down to broken stems, in *Ophelia*, and the 'marvel of perfection in drawing' of the foliage in *Ferdinand and Ariel* – delighted her. Beside such clarity, other paintings faded, like Holman Hunt's *The Light of the World*, viewed on a visit to Oxford when Beatrix was seventeen: 'The details I was much disappointed with, there is no particularly careful and minute work as in Millais's Pre-Raphaelite pictures.'[18]

A guidebook to the Tate Gallery, published in 1898, claimed that, while working on *Ophelia*, Millais had been seen 'applying a magnifying glass to the branch of a tree he was painting, in order to study closely the veins of the leaves'. In spirit it was the very approach Beatrix herself adopted, beginning with microscopic studies at her desk in Bolton Gardens. In a carefully annotated study of branches of sweet bay painted much later, in 1900, she noted the direction of sunlight striking the leaves and the extent of the transparency of leaf veins without sunlight. A desire to understand and to explain nature (an aim common to Victorian amateur scientists) influenced her from early on; equally important was her dislike of the element of caricature that too often marred the kind of anthropomorphic pictures of animals she began painting in her mid-twenties. 'When I was young it was still the fashion to admire Pre-Raphaelites,' she acknowledged in 1943. She drew attention to the Pre-Raphaelites' 'meticulous copying of flowers & plants' and 'their somewhat niggling but absolutely genuine admiration for copying natural details'; 'the real essence of Pre-Raphaelite art', she considered, was focus.[19] Cecily Parsley's harvest of cowslips heaped on stone flags, each golden flowerhead scored with darker gold, the embroidered poppies and cornflowers of the Mayor of Gloucester's waistcoat and the rainbow of pansies, peonies and rhododendrons in Tom Kitten's garden, all suggest Beatrix's debt to the minute botanical details of Millais's early paintings. Until her sight worsened in middle age, close focus and truth to nature were hallmarks of her painting, and she always aimed at accuracy.

By contrast, her dislike of Rossetti's painting, with its dreamlike sensuousness and lush stylisation, arose from a suspicion that artificiality could never be truly beautiful.[20] *Her* work, she asserted in time, 'succeeded by being absolutely matter-of-fact'.[21]

Her diary records Millais calling on Rupert for landscape photographs. Among requests the latter was unable to satisfy were photographs of an apple tree in 1882 for the orchard in *Pomona* and, two years later, a running stream for *An Idyll of 1745*.[22] Beatrix herself painted from life. Her preliminary sketch survives for Pigling Bland and Alexander's crossroads, with fingerpost and five-bar gate; so does her sketch of the garden, dense with snapdragons, in front of Buckle Yeat Cottage, Near Sawrey, in which Duchess reads Ribby's invitation to tea in *The Tale of the Pie and the Patty-Pan*. She borrowed the china on the Tailor of Gloucester's dresser from the cobbler's wife at Near Sawrey and studied details of eighteenth-century dress in the South Kensington Museum.[23] In 1909, progress on *The Tale of Timmy Tiptoes* was held up by Beatrix's need to visit London Zoo to see for herself a bear at close quarters; in the same story she modelled Chippy Hackee on a real chipmunk belonging to a cousin.[24] Two black Pomeranians posed for Duchess: Beatrix borrowed them for sittings from their owner, Mrs Rogerson, and also photographed the dogs to prove to publishers Frederick Warne & Co. the accuracy of her portrayal.

From her first efforts, painted at the nursery table, nature and art marched hand in hand. Art provided a means of scrutinising and rationalising the natural world; nature supplied subjects for Beatrix's – and Bertram's – painting. 'A willow bush,' Beatrix pronounced at nineteen, 'is as beautiful as the *human form divine*', though, as it happened, notably less challenging to Beatrix, who never mastered drawing the human figure and wisely did her best to avoid including figures in her books.[25] Beatrix's subjects when she and Bertram taught themselves transfer printing included dogs, a horse, a dormouse and a family of rabbits. Eventually she would conclude that, of these, only mice and rabbits lay really firmly within her scope: 'I can manage to describe little rubbish, like mice and rabbits – dogs, sheep and horses are on a higher level.'[26] Horses, like humans, are mostly absent from her work.

When Bertram went away to prep school at The Grange in Eastbourne in 1883, Beatrix used his microscope to further her study of insects. She taught herself how to prepare slides for the microscope and recorded what she saw with utmost precision, using a dry-brush watercolour technique to outline every gossamer filament. Under highest magnification, she depicted the coloured scales on the wings of tortoiseshell butterflies – bright tesserae like the soft mosaic pattern of Victorian rag rugs; she painted the segmental legs, the head and thorax of ground beetles and a sheet web spider in all its mottled glory; a spider crab, ticks, a mite as rosy and rounded as a potato; damselflies, spiders, ants, a tarantula and the privet hawkmoth. She discovered tiny, transparent organisms in pond water, including water fleas; she transferred those too to the viewing plate for painting. Her approach was forensic and, with a mixture of determination and ironic self-awareness, she arranged her studies to resemble the plates of scientific handbooks rather than the watercolour musings of a lady amateur.

As a child, she painted everything from caterpillars to a hippopotamus, omnivorous in her appetite. Over time she specialised: after entomology, paleontology and mycology. Her obsession with fungi, starting in a small way in 1887, resulted in her finding and painting a number of little-known species and, ultimately, a theory – since challenged – about reproduction through spore germination in members of the *Agaricineae* family. Along the way she completed more than 300 studies of British fungi, several among the finest of her paintings. After her death a selection were chosen to illustrate Walter Findlay's *Wayside & Woodland Fungi*.

Not for Beatrix, then, 'very queer' carnations or 'rather

queer' holly. What she called 'the careful botanical studies of my youth' eventually comprised an extensive informal florilegium: wild flowers, including cotton sedge, cuckoo flower, dead nettle, sea lavender and wild yellow balsam; of garden flowers, dahlias, tiger lilies, pansies, tulips and carnations. Her sketches of foxgloves would be recycled to sinister effect in *The Tale of Jemima Puddle-Duck* or fringing stiles in *The Tale of Mrs Tiggy-Winkle*; in *The Tale of Benjamin Bunny*, carnations line steps in Mr McGregor's garden. Exactingness was as much a feature of Beatrix's character as her parents'. It surfaced first in her painting and afterwards in her approach to her books. It played its part, too, in her fiction – in Tom Titmouse, in *The Tale of Mrs Tiggy-Winkle*, 'most terrible particular' about his 'little dicky shirt-fronts'; the Miss Goldfinches at The Contented Siskin coffee tavern in *The Tale of Little Pig Robinson*, with their 'spotlessly clean' tables and china; above all, in the story of that 'most terribly tidy particular little mouse', Mrs Tittlemouse, whose life is a study in housewifely punctilio.

Despite – or because of – their opposition to Beatrix making friends of her own age, Rupert and Helen Potter had fewer objections to pets. Sandy the cairn terrier was succeeded by a spaniel called Spot, acquired at Dalguise. At intervals the children's nursery resembled a menagerie. A drawing by Beatrix, made in 1885 when she was nineteen, shows a tortoise in front of the fire grate and, on a table close by, two typically tiny Victorian birdcages, each with its feathered prisoner. Adjacent stands a collector's cabinet like one she had looked for with her parents the previous winter in Mr Cutter's furniture shop near the British Museum.[27] From the moment Bertram was old enough to accompany Beatrix in her searches, the siblings set about cramming its shallow drawers with butterflies, moths and beetles, stones, shells, fossils, even old musket shot. In addition they filled their third-floor rooms with animals, from reptiles to raptors. A robin lacking tail feathers, bought by Beatrix from a pet shop, was a temporary resident. Speedily she returned it to freedom in the flower walk in Kensington Gardens, 'where it hopped into aucuba laurel with great satisfaction'.[28]

In September 1884, Beatrix surprised herself by the pleasure she took in looking after Bertram's bat, following his return to school: 'It is a charming little creature, quite tame and apparently happy as long as it has sufficient flies and raw meat.'[29] She observed its habits, as she had previously newts' breathing, and noted the use it made of its legs and its tail. When the bat died, Beatrix followed Bertram's instructions on how to stuff and preserve it, taking careful measurements in the interests of verisimilitude. Of course she painted it too.

Her attitude to nature lacked squeamishness. Animals that died were boiled, stripped of fur and flesh and reassembled as skeletons; she inserted glass eyes into cleaned skulls. At Dalguise, aged thirteen, she drew a dead siskin; she made a series of watercolour studies of a thrush 'picked up dead in the snow'. Beatrix referred to what she called 'our little bone-cupboards', where skeletons were safely stored. On one occasion careless dusting resulted in a shower of mouse bones landing on her head. 'I caught the skeleton of a favourite dormouse,' she wrote, 'but six others were broken and mixed. I mended them all up. I thought it a curious instance of the beautifully minute differences and fittings together of the bones.'[30] As a child at Camfield, she helped prepare a favourite farm animal for the table: 'scrap[ing] the smiling countenance of my own grandmother's deceased pig, with scalding water and the sharp-edged bottom of a brass candle-stick.'[31] Remembering that experience in 1911, she felt moved to protest against the Protection of Animals Act, which proposed preventing children under sixteen from gaining access to slaughterhouses. Her attitude was that of the scientist or countrywoman; she mostly lacked sentiment. The 'matter of fact' quality she admired in her stories was a workaday briskness. There is no elaboration, for example, to Mrs Rabbit's statement that Peter's father ended his life in a pie, and we are intended to laugh at the admission of Ginger the tom cat, in *The Tale of Ginger and Pickles*, that serving mice 'made his mouth water'.

Housed in the Potter nursery at one time or another were a pair of lizards, Toby and Judy, bought at the seaside at Ilfracombe, salamanders and 'a little ring-snake only fourteen inches long... [that] hissed like fun and tied itself into knots', which the children called Sally.[32] There was a green budgerigar, a canary, an owl that bit the heads off dead mice and hooted all night and, improbably, a kestrel and a jay belonging to Bertram. The last two were of doubtful domesticity and Beatrix reported the jay killing one of Bertram's bats 'in a disgusting fashion'.[33] Judy was Beatrix's model on at least three occasions, including in an illustration she made for *Alice's Adventures in Wonderland*: surrounded by ministering guinea pigs, Judy lies on her back, limbs cruciform, as 'The little Lizard, Bill'.[34] Sally's sojourn in the schoolroom proved brief: along with four black newts she escaped after only two nights. Two of the newts were recovered, but Sally's disappearance proved final.

By contrast, a green frog called Punch, acquired when Beatrix was about twelve, remained with the siblings for more than five years. In 1882, Beatrix found a snail she called Old Bill. For a year she collected snails, housing them in a single plant pot. All were given names by the sixteen-year-old: Lord and Lady Salisbury, Mars and Venus, Mr and Mrs Camfield. When all died, in December 1883, after Beatrix failed to provide them with water, she described her loss without irony as 'an awful tragedy'.[35]

Unsurprisingly she grew adept and fearless at handling animals; she had none of the diffidence or anxiety little Lucie exhibits in Mrs Tiggy-winkle's kitchen. 'I seem to be able to tame any sort of animal,' she wrote.[36] Among her conquests were the female hedgehog who inspired her fictional namesake, Mrs Tiggy, 'just like a very fat, rather stupid little dog', who 'lived in the house a long time'.[37] 'She was not a bit prickly with me, she used to lay her prickles flat back to be stroked.'[38] Again Beatrix made detailed notes on the hedgehog's habits, including the onset of hibernation. Having watched 'the somewhat ghastly process' by which Mrs Tiggy achieved the necessary catalepsis, Beatrix concluded 'the hibernating trance is entirely under the animal's own control, and only in a secondary degree dependent on the weather'.[39]

Beatrix loved mice. She reported that she was 'always catching & taming' them: 'the common wild ones are far more intelligent & amusing than the fancy variety'.[40] A mouse called Hunca Munca – as dauntless as Tom Thumb's wife in *The Tale of Two Bad Mice* – disgraced itself by nibbling a circular hole through one of Beatrix's sheets, but otherwise displayed all the adroitness of a well-trained circus animal. 'I used to let it run about in the evenings & when I wanted to catch it I flapped a pocket handkcf in the middle of the room – or rooms – when it would come out and fight, leaping at the hdcf.'[41] Another mouse trapped itself inside the hollow brass curtain pole of Beatrix's bedroom at Camfield. Later, a less adventurous 'little brown mouse' called Dusty ran about on Beatrix's table as she wrote letters.[42]

On account of her sleepiness, Beatrix's favourite mouse was named Xarifa after the 'Zegri lady', or Muslim maiden, of a popular poem by Walter Scott's son-in-law John Gibson Lockhart, *The Bridal of Andalla*. (In the poem, Xarifa is repeatedly implored to 'rise up', a suitable command for a sleepy dormouse, though Beatrix substituted 'wake up' for 'rise up'.) Xarifa the dormouse died of asthma and old age in the autumn of 1886. Her eyebrows and nose were white; she was completely blind. Beatrix described her as 'the sweetest little animal I ever knew'.[43] Rupert had photographed her sitting on Beatrix's outstretched palm. More than forty years later, Beatrix remembered Xarifa in *The Fairy Caravan*: 'Her nose and eyebrows were turning grey; she was a most sweet person, but slumberous.'[44]

She felt a similar affection for a white rat called Sammy, acquired when he was already old and very fat; like Xarifa, he too proved a sleepy pet. But he was not above mischief: 'he was a bit of a thief... I used to find all sorts of things hidden in his box.'[45] Sammy had a trick of rolling a hard-boiled egg along the floor of the third-floor passages that Beatrix remembered in *The Tale of Samuel Whiskers*. She replaced the egg then with a rolling pin.

Beatrix's first experience of rabbits was in the wild at Dalguise and Camfield. An early rabbit, Tommy, may have been caught wild and tamed; ditto a 'painfully nervous' female called Mopsy,[46] the rabbit she painted at thirteen – a slightly stiff study, with very dry paint used to suggest the texture of fur – and Josephine, called 'Josey', whom she drew stealing oatcakes from a tin in a letter to Angela, Denis and Clare Mackail in January 1903.

In 1890 she bought a rabbit from a pet shop; she smuggled him home in a paper bag and christened him Benjamin H. Bouncer. She set to work drawing 'noisy cheerful' Benjamin and covered a sheet of paper with studies of his head, viewed from every angle. He proved a capricious animal: fond of peppermints, cabbage and gooseberries and with 'an appetite for certain sorts of paint',[47] 'at one moment amiably sentimental to the verge of silliness', equally capable of the opposite. 'He used to bang his hind-legs & rump against the wire fender in the school room as "he frisked around".'[48] He became the model for Peter

Rabbit, whom Beatrix remembered later as 'drawn from a very intelligent Belgian hare called Bounce'.[49]

Benjamin was succeeded by Peter, 'bought at a very tender age, in the Uxbridge Road, Shepherds Bush [sic], for the exorbitant sum of 4/6';[50] afterwards she could not remember why she called him Peter.[51] Like the Peter Rabbit of her tales, the real Peter was more timorous than Benjamin; he was calmer, biddable, 'generally asleep before the fire'.[52] 'His disposition was uniformly amiable and his temper unfailingly sweet.'[53] Beatrix sketched him awake and asleep; in August 1899 she painted him 'on an old quilt made of scraps of flannel and blue cloth which he always lay on' in front of the nursery hearth.[54] In a drawing called *The Rabbit's Dream*, Peter dreams of sleeping in the half-tester bed in Bedroom 4 at Camfield Place, which had once been Beatrix's room. The dreaming Peter forms the picture's central vignette: around it is a border of smaller drawings of sleeping rabbits. Beatrix may have been inspired by Robert Buss's popular painting of 1875, *Dickens' Dream*, in which a sleeping Dickens is surrounded by characters from his novels. In time the success of *The Tale of Peter Rabbit*, and the pressure she felt from her publishers to produce sequels, changed Beatrix's attitude towards rabbits. Before that, indulgent of their shortcomings, she described them as 'creatures of warm volatile temperament but shallow and absurdly transparent', and their warmth, as well as their shallowness, entertained her through periods alone in the nursery after Bertram's departure.[55] Following Peter's death on 26 January 1901, Beatrix described him simply as 'an affectionate companion and a quiet friend'.[56]

More than any of Beatrix's pets, rabbits proved receptive to simple training, albeit inconsistently so. When hungry, Peter was adept at tricks: 'jumping (stick, hands, hoop, back and forward), ringing a little bell and drumming on a tambourine.'[57] Benjamin consented to be walked on a leather dog lead. Like Pig Robinson walking hand in hand with a sailor, this spectacle, Beatrix reported, 'seemed to cause unbounded amusement' to all who witnessed it.[58]

Few of Beatrix's schoolroom menagerie were formally sanctioned by her parents. With something approaching triumph, the twenty-three-year-old recorded that, following his purchase, Benjamin's existence 'was not observed by the nursery authorities for a week'.[59] Nevertheless the Potters cannot have failed to be aware of the 'secret' denizens of the third floor, regularly smuggled up- and downstairs for more or less successful airings in the garden. In Benjamin's case, there were no repercussions and he later acquired an outdoor hutch. Photographs indicate that, probably as a result, either Rupert or Helen decided to protect their flowerbeds with wire netting. Other animals met with less favourable responses. Helen Potter was vocal in her dislike of Bertram's jay: 'Mamma expressed her uncharitable hope that we might have seen the last of it,' Beatrix wrote, after a journey in which the bird kicked at its travelling case and 'swore'.[60]

Despite their failure to recognise their children's need for friends, Rupert and Helen Potter understood the companionship Beatrix and Bertram derived from their pets, an emotional outlet they otherwise lacked. Beatrix's journal records time spent with her cousins, like her visit to the National Gallery with sisters Kate and Jessy Potter in the spring of 1882, but no time spent alone with her immediate contemporaries outside the family. Instead, of the company of Judy the lizard, she wrote, 'I have had a great deal of pleasure from that little Creature.'[61] She was eighteen, an age when the thoughts of other girls of her class could reasonably have been expected to be directed towards marriage. Significant among Beatrix's impressions of her last governess, Annie Carter, who replaced Miss Hammond when Beatrix was seventeen and Miss Carter herself only twenty, is her statement that Annie Carter 'was one of the youngest people I have ever seen'.[62]

Until that point Beatrix's life had been lived among her parents' and grandparents' contemporaries. She had not had opportunities for disputing and rejecting inherited views in company with her peers (although her journal offers many examples of her refusal to accept parental shibboleths unchallenged). Little wonder she set stories in the past: the Tailor of Gloucester struggles to make a living 'in the time of swords and periwigs and full-skirted coats with flowered lappets'; Jeremy Fisher wears knee breeches and the cutaway coats of a Regency buck. The recent past was every bit as alive to Beatrix as her collection of tamed wildlife – in her grandmother's tales of Crompton family history, overheard beneath the library table at Camfield; in John Bright's reminiscences of prison reformer Elizabeth Fry, whom he had known well; in Nurse McKenzie's folklore, *The Lady of the Lake* and the 'Waverley' novels; in Millais's reinvention of history in a succession of winsomely populist paintings; and especially at Dalguise, where 'the Lords and Ladies of the last century walked with me along the overgrown paths, and picked the old fashioned flowers among the box and rose hedges of the garden.'[63] The past was a default setting for Beatrix's imagination: she was reassured by its familiarity and seduced by its narrative possibilities.

The significance of Beatrix Potter's schoolroom menagerie extends beyond the self-proclaimed 'thoroughness' of her nature study. In her stories, characters are simultaneously animal and human, like Ginger and Pickles: 'the people who kept the shop. Ginger was a yellow tom-cat, and Pickles was a terrier.' Distinctions are fluid: double identity is both asserted and denied. Jemima Puddle-duck finds 'mighty civil and handsome' the 'elegantly dressed gentleman... with black prick ears and sandy coloured whiskers', and the reader does not challenge the incompatibility of the human traits of civility and elegant dressing with an animal's black prick ears. Older readers recognise Mrs Tiggy-winkle as a hedgehog; for younger readers, like Lucie in the story, the washerwoman's identity is less certain, confused by human clothes, speech, occupation.

This attitude to her imaginary animals was one Beatrix developed in her nursery dealings with her pets once she was left alone in the schoolroom after Bertram's departure. Then her interest ceased to be either fully artistic or scientific. Rabbits, mice, hedgehogs filled a void. Beatrix looked for, and found in them, human quirks and habits, even training Mrs Tiggy to drink milk from a miniature teacup. Unselfconsciously she introduced Xarifa the dormouse to Potter family friends, including Millais and Bright. And afterwards Benjamin Bouncer featured in her dreams. Of a restless night in May 1890, she wrote that she 'had an impression [in the small hours of the night] that Bunny came to my bedside in a white cotton nightcap and tickled me with his whiskers.'[64]

Forced into protracted girlhood by her parents' refusal

to condone any measure of independence for their adult daughter, and cut off from friends of her own age, Beatrix played games on her hands and knees with the mouse she called Hunca Munca; with a pair of garden scissors, she clipped Peter's toenails;[65] she dreamt of being tickled by Benjamin's whiskers in her bed. Her pets became the inseparable companions of her twenties and recipients of unfocused emotions. Benjamin and Hunca Munca travelled with her by train, contained within 'a covered basket' and a 'small old box'; she travelled with Mrs Tiggy the hedgehog and, on different occasions, two birds' skeletons and a container filled with eleven minnows.[66] Of visits to her married cousin Edith at Melford Hall in Suffolk, Edith's son Willie remembered his excitement at Beatrix's arrival, 'for she always brought a cage with mice, another with a hamster or a porcupine, and a third with something else in it'.[67] At moments of need, 'the rabbit hutch [was] a great resource', serviceable as an additional trunk.[68] Beatrix's actions had ceased to be dictated by a naturalist's curiosity – and the paintings of her pets she went on to produce rejected the would-be scientific aspect of her microscope studies of insect life. Anthropomorphism is the hallmark of Beatrix's published work: animals with human characteristics. It was a habit of mind formed of necessity, the creative legacy of her isolation.

'I have had so much pleasure from that box,' Beatrix wrote in February 1904 to her publisher Norman Warne, whom she thanked for making 'a little house' for her mice. 'I am never tired of watching them run up & down.'[69] Even as she approached her thirty-eighth birthday, Beatrix remained absorbed by her mice.

On the western shore of Lake Windermere, high above the water close to the lake's northernmost tip, Rupert and Helen Potter, with Beatrix, Bertram and Spot, arrived in the summer of 1882. Their destination was a crenelated greystone house, Wray Castle; they stayed from the second week in July until the end of October. Miss Hammond arrived later.

Built in the 1840s by a Liverpool doctor whose wife, Margaret Preston, had inherited a distilling fortune, this cumbersome structure of towers and mock arrow slits was Rupert's solution to the prohibitive increase that year in the rental cost of Dalguise. Like Dalguise, Wray Castle offered fishing; there was boating on the lake and, for Beatrix and Bertram, at sixteen and ten, unexplored walks and natural specimens that included a Douglas pine Beatrix labelled 'one of the finest in England'.[70] Timber felling by previous owners had left parts of the park sparsely planted; close by there were damson, plum and walnut trees, elder thickets, a handful of towering beeches and a mulberry bush planted by Wordsworth. Long views stretched across the hills and the water. By the time the Potters returned to London, autumn cast across the country the rusty amber glow that Beatrix later captured in the Derwentwater setting of her illustrations to *The Tale of Squirrel Nutkin*: 'the nuts were ripe, and the leaves on the hazel bushes were golden and green'. She always preferred the autumn. The holiday at Wray convinced her it was 'far away the best time at the Lakes'.[71]

Her journal is silent about her response to the heavy-weight architectural fantasy that is Wray Castle, though later she would claim that 'Victorian architects... did more mischief than Hitler'.[72] Building costs, she noted, were rumoured at £60,000; the architect drank himself to death before completion. Beatrix's painting of the library – red walls and timbered ceiling – shows a room of earnest decorative historicism. Rooms contained their fill of the old oak furniture Beatrix always loved: two years later, in an antiques shop in Oxford, she coveted an oak cupboard priced at six pounds that reminded her of one at Wray.[73] Exposed to changeable weather, the Potters explored the vicinity on foot and by carriage; they visited Hawkshead and Coniston, village churches, local beauty spots. Inevitably

Rupert took photographs – the slow, precise preserving of memories. Beatrix missed Dalguise. After eleven summers, the change of holiday destination felt like a severance from the past. Yet there were unexpected intimations that her fledgling connection to the Lake District ran as deep as her passion for the Highlands. 'Papa found a lock of hair in an old album here on a bit of paper,' she wrote on 21 July. The paper dated from the school days of Margaret Preston. It stated 'that the lock of hair was cut from the head of Fanny, 4th daughter of Abraham Crompton of Chorley Hall,' Beatrix's maternal great-grandfather.[74]

The Potters returned to the Lake District throughout the next decade. Five times they based themselves at Lingholm, Colonel Kemp's house on the banks of Derwentwater near Keswick; on other occasions Rupert took a house in Near Sawrey called Lakefield. In May 1884, Rupert suggested a return to Dalguise. Beatrix's response surprised her. 'I feel an extraordinary dislike to this idea, a childish dislike, but the memory of that home is the only bit of childhood I have left.'[75] With the parting from Scotland she had forcibly – and painfully – let go a part of herself. The break with childhood holiday routine and its memories of intense happiness discomfited Beatrix and she had no desire to un-settle cherished memories with an altered reality. Ten days later, she returned to the fray: 'I cannot bear to see it again.

How times and I have changed!'[76] She referred to Dalguise as 'home' and dreaded the spell breaking. Homecoming, she knew, was beyond her adult self.

To Dalguise the Potters duly went, arriving on 27 May. Inevitably Beatrix lamented its changed aspect – 'a horrid telegraph wire up to the house through the avenue, a Saw-Mill opposite the house'[77] – though the changes lay as much within herself. She was susceptible to landscape. Once Dalguise had made her spirits soar; now there were signs it might drag her down. Although there would be further Scottish holidays, she would discover that her consolation lay in the Lake District.

· 4 ·

'Matters of complaint'

Beatrix was fourteen when her father photographed her with Spot the spaniel on holiday in Scotland at Dalguise House.

'Tom Kitten did not want to be
shut up in a cupboard'

The Tale of Samuel Whiskers, 1908

'I HAVE PERSEVERED in nothing for more than a week at a time except toothache,' Beatrix wrote at the end of 1886.[1] Much of the year had passed her by, hostage to illness. She felt weak, 'unsettled', 'demoralised'. For six months she had been unable to write her journal. There had been bouts of sickness; she felt tired continually.

The following spring, away again in the Lake District, a swollen ankle turned out to be rheumatic fever. The holiday was cut short and, for three weeks in London, Beatrix was confined to bed. 'Could not be turned... without screaming out,' she remembered. The pain settled in her legs. Maddeningly it moved 'backwards and forwards, up and down each leg, never in more than one place at a time.' After a fortnight, she was still only well enough to be lifted onto a sofa for two hours each afternoon. She was treated with hot flannels, camphor and quinine.[2]

The atmosphere in Bolton Gardens became frazzled. Helen reached 'her wits end', a response that may or may not suggest sympathy for her daughter. For his part, Rupert was worrying about Bertram, who had taken a violent dislike to his public school, Charterhouse, from his first term, in the autumn of 1886. He had since contracted pleurisy. Bertram's pleurisy, added to an outbreak of diphtheria which killed the school matron, forced Rupert reluctantly to withdraw his son, who returned instead to The Grange. Millais sent Beatrix 'a little note when I was in bed with the rheumatics, take the world as we find it'.[3] Even at this stage she needed few lessons in stoicism.

Beatrix was accustomed to feeling unwell. Colds and headaches had dogged her childhood. Like Miss Matilda Pussycat in *The Fairy Caravan*, she was prone to neuralgia, with its stabbing pains in the head and the neck; like Chippy Hackee in *The Tale of Timmy Tiptoes*, she suffered from head colds. On 22 February 1883, she had noted in her journal, 'Have had a cold most of the time since Christmas... Think it's going to stop till Easter';[4] the year ended as it had begun with bad colds again.[5] Before then, an unexplained lump on her right wrist provoked a mixed response of anxiety and irritation. In November the doctor pricked and drained it, leaving her temporarily without the use of her right hand.[6] She described her head as 'uncertain'[7] – dizzy and painful:

she was no stranger to the sensation. Her mother would describe her as 'apt to be sick and to faint'.[8]

Unable to understand or control her debilitation, Beatrix marvelled at those more fortunate than herself. Fashionable society women – corseted, primped but busy – became objects of her fascination. In her journal she asked, 'How is it these high-heeled ladies who dine out, paint and pinch their waists to deformity, can racket about all day long, while I who sleep o' nights, can turn in my stays, and dislike sweets and dinners, am so tired towards the end of the afternoon that I can scarcely keep my feet?'[9] Her attitude was one of puzzled envy rather than admiration and the feelings of exhaustion that overwhelmed her were real enough.

In March 1885, when Beatrix was nineteen, her hair was cut off. Previously it had reached to within inches of her knees. 'I may say without pride that I have seldom seen a more beautiful head of hair than mine,' she commented wistfully after it was gone; she described herself as having 'a red nose and a shorn head'.[10] Over preceding months illness had caused much of her hair to fall out: the hair-dresser's task was simply one of tidying up.[11] Like Timmy Willie's 'insignificant' tail in *The Tale of Johnny Town-Mouse*, her cropped head, so at odds with current hairdressing fashions, was an indignity to Beatrix and, Samson-like,

81

she experienced a sense of diminishment. As a curiosity, Rupert photographed his daughter with her 'shorn head'. Neither Beatrix nor her parents understood that her hair would never grow back completely.

Two months later, Rupert was unamused by an incident at the International Inventions Exhibition. 'Since my hair is cut my hats won't stick on,' Beatrix explained. A gust swept her hat clean off her head into a fountain, causing 'immense amusement' to bystanders but 'consternation' to Rupert. Clearly his response did not spare Beatrix's feelings. 'I always thought I was born to be a discredit to my parents, but it was exhibited in a marked manner today,' she stated baldly. The breezy matter-of-factness of her tone failed her: 'he does not often take me out, and I doubt he will do it again for a long time.'[12] Aside from illness, Beatrix was plagued by a lack of confidence.

In Beatrix's books incomplete families and poor parenting are the norm. Peter Rabbit, Tom Kitten and Pigling Bland are fatherless. Jemima Puddle-duck is on course to prove herself an inadequate mother and Tabitha Twitchit is an 'anxious parent', who oscillates between affronted firmness and complete lack of control. Despite affectionate natures, Benjamin Bunny and Flopsy suggest a degree of irresponsibility. Pig Robinson lives with his aunts Dorcas and Porcas, whose surrogacy wants vigilance. In the absence both of mother and father, Squirrel Nutkin and Twinkleberry embody stereotypes of the 'good' and 'bad' sibling; Nutkin lacks discipline and craves attention. Tom Thumb and Hunca Munca seem unlikely to impress upon their offspring clear notions of right and wrong.

Insofar as they acknowledge that animals do not typically live in nuclear families, the tales reflect truth to nature. Added to this, parentlessness is a conceit of children's literature: in many stories, lack of parental supervision is essential to the plot. In Beatrix's carefully crafted fictions, her focus on flawed parenting indicates more than a desire for realism. From a reasonably young age, her attitude to her own parents included ambivalence and, often, exasperation.

By the time she was fourteen, she had begun a secret diary. Late in life, in her only known reference to the journal, she explained her motives as 'a united admiration of Boswell and Pepys' and 'the itch to write, without having any material to write about'.[13] Within the journal itself, her only reference to 'common' Pepys is disparaging; it seems more likely that Beatrix was inspired by Pepys's use of private cipher than the substance of his diary.

From her first entry, she devised a code of her own to

protect her journal from prying eyes. This clandestine quality added to the enjoyment of the undertaking, which she maintained, in a series of ordinary lined exercise books, on and off for sixteen years. 'I used to write long-winded descriptions, hymns (!) and records of conversations,' Beatrix explained in old age. She chronicled current affairs, faithfully reproducing Rupert's commentary; and she noted down humorous anecdotes gleaned from magazines and newspapers, like the story of the servant in a Continental hotel, who 'copied down [a] gentleman's name from his portmanteau': 'Mr Warranted Solid Matter'.[14] The journal records holidays, scenery, natural history. There are apparently verbatim reports of conversations and pains-taking transcriptions of her grandmother and great-aunts' reminiscences. The business of memory itself recurs, Beatrix asserting the crispness of her own recall, which included memories of learning to walk and learning to read. She lingered over memories of her childhood, insisting on happiness past. Recording memory – confining it within words and giving it concrete shape on the page – was one way Beatrix sought to control her self-identity.

Throughout the journal self-assessment is intermit-tent. Beatrix deals briskly with references to her state of mind; her pauses for reflection are relatively few. At times her meaning is elusive, as if she struggles to make sense of her shifting moods. Her description of 1884, for example, is clogged with contradictions: 'So cold and stormy, and yet such gleams of peace and light making the darkness stranger and more dreary.'[15] Instead, the journal impresses upon the reader, in details that are more often implied than explicit, striking portraits of Rupert and Helen Potter and intimations of a gulf between parents and child. Of the Potters' twentieth wedding anniversary in 1883, for example, Beatrix comments laconically: 'They have been married twenty years today.'[16] There is an unaffectionate quality to that starkly unadorned pronoun, 'they'. Equally marked are the journal's indications of Beatrix's own strength of character. She emerges as a young woman engaged in a struggle for self-determinism. Her desire to decide the course of her life is stubborn and her wish to dedicate herself entirely to her painting an unorthodox aspiration within the Potters' studiedly conformist milieu. It seems unlikely that Beatrix confided these hopes fully to her parents, particularly her mother, whose behaviour points to a conventional approach to sexual politics, or that she failed to understand the circumscribed nature of female independence in a conservative household of the 1880s. And her ideas remained unresolved. She longed for the freedom to decide her own course: she was sufficiently her parents' daughter to 'hold an old-fashioned notion that a happy marriage is the crown of a woman's life', although almost certain to involve at least partial surrender of the free choice she craved.[17] Even as she clamoured for independence and control in the matter of her painting, the Beatrix of her twenties was, like her parents, instinctively conservative.

Her reaction to a portrait betrays something of her state of mind. In 1882, Beatrix's cousin Kate, the eldest of the three daughters of Rupert's eldest brother, Crompton Potter, sat for Briton Rivière. Beatrix was sixteen, her near contemporary Kate acknowledged as the beauty of the family. Rivière's hefty fee of £1,000 reflected his status, according to Beatrix, as 'one of the foremost living artists' – and presumably the esteem in which Kate's father, who collected paintings by Rivière, held his pretty daughter.[18]

His portrait of Kate Potter includes her black poodle Figaro and a lively pug. Handsomely dressed in red and black, she stands in front of an old oak court cupboard. With one hand she makes to open the upper door, while the dogs wait in lively expectation. Beatrix took exception to the pug. She considered the figure of Kate poorly painted.

For once Beatrix was in full agreement with her parents. Exhibited at the Royal Academy that summer, *Cupboard Love* provoked in this prickly and socially ambitious couple a degree of chagrin. 'After all one has heard, it is not as bad as I expected,' Beatrix reflected in her journal. Then the twist of the knife: 'Should not have known Kate, but it is rather a pretty picture. The chief part of it, however, is taken up by the cupboard.'[19] She returned to the fray two years later when, following Crompton Potter's death, his paintings were sold at auction: 'Rivière certainly does not draw figures well. He took a great deal of trouble over Kate, and was very well satisfied with it, but it certainly is not good.'[20] With faintest possible praise, she described it as 'a smooth neat picture'.[21] Her reaction was acidulated in its contempt.

The cause of Beatrix's irritation, however, differed from that of her parents. She understood Kate's portrait as a rite of passage, a public acknowledgement of adulthood. Three years later, to Beatrix's consternation and Rupert's horror, Kate became engaged to a Captain Cruikshank, without fortune or family and not a Unitarian. 'I can't understand the girl not having more self-pride or ambition... Love in a cottage is sentimental, but the parties must be very pleasing to each other to make it tolerable,' Beatrix commented tellingly in her journal; for his part, Rupert was 'grieved and exasperated to tears'.[22] The same autumn, Kate's sister Blanche and another Potter cousin, Emily, also accepted proposals of marriage, both more 'suitable' than Kate's. But Beatrix remained on the third floor at Bolton Gardens, temporarily at loggerheads with her parents over

her future. So far was she from matrimony that wearily
she described her mother's warnings against marrying
a cousin – Emily Potter's case – as 'an unnecessary precaution'.[23] 'I may be lonely, but better that than an unhappy
marriage,' she consoled herself without conviction.[24] By her
mid-twenties Beatrix was so lonely that she invented an
imaginary friend, Esther, to whom she addressed lengthy
disquisitions in her journal, influenced by her reading of
eighteenth-century novelist and diarist Fanny Burney. Her
riposte came later, in *The Tale of the Pie and the Patty-Pan*,
when Duchess searches Ribby's cupboards. In an illustration entitled 'Where is the pie made of mouse?', Beatrix
revisited Rivière's painting. Like Kate, Duchess is presented
to the viewer in profile.

The period following Bertram's departure for boarding
school in April 1883 had proved unusually challenging for
Beatrix. Within a week of his absence, she was using her
journal as a repository for fluctuating emotions. 'I am up
one day and down another. Have been a long way down
today, and now my head feels empty and I am nothing
particular.'[25] She was months short of her seventeenth
birthday. Miss Hammond's tenure in the schoolroom was
over: she had no more to impart. Beatrix interpreted her

removal as a sign that her formal education was at an end. From now on, she would be free to pursue her own course of study, centred on her art: 'I thought to have set in view German, English Reading, and General Knowledge, cutting off more and more time for painting.'[26] She did not anticipate the extent to which she would miss the governess who, for eleven years, had been her constant companion. Nor did she regret unduly her parting from her first art teacher, Miss Cameron, in May.

But Helen had other ideas. Without consulting her daughter, she had appointed Annie Carter as Beatrix's new governess; Miss Hammond would remain in touch with the household at 2 Bolton Gardens. Beatrix was disappointed. Like Tom Thumb and Hunca Munca thwarted by the plaster ham on the doll's house dining table – the pudding, the lobster, the pears and the oranges – her disappointment led to anger. 'If they said I must, I'd do it willingly enough, only my temper'd be very nasty,' she wrote.[27] She concluded that Rupert would not force her to remain in the schoolroom, and blamed her mother. Helen may have attempted to placate Beatrix. The new arrangement, she reassured her, was for a year only. Miss Carter stayed till July 1885, when, unexpectedly, she left to get married.

In the event, any placating was done by Miss Carter herself. Beatrix came to regard her last governess as her best, and the women remained friends following Annie Carter's marriage to Edwin Moore and removal to married homes in Bayswater then Wandsworth Common. And schoolroom lessons were only part of the problem. Bertram was Beatrix's junior by six years. His companionship had prolonged the illusion of childhood. With Bertram gone, that illusion vanished as completely as visits to sail his model boats on the Round Pond or in the gardens of the Horticultural Society; like holidays at Dalguise, a chapter of Beatrix's life was over. Yet she remained in the school-room: Miss Carter's presence was proof of that. Was she a child, then, or an adult? 'Is this being a grown-up?' she asked in her journal.[28]

Her uncertainty was genuine. She was struggling with a series of losses: Bertram, Miss Hammond, her own private Eden at Dalguise, and the deaths of two of her grandparents, Edmund Potter, in October 1883, and Jane Leech the following year. The combined effect was to detach Beatrix from her childhood, without offering her any compensations of adulthood. Hers remained an existence without autonomy: a sense of her own powerlessness contributed to her anxiety. She mistrusted her mother. Sporadically she felt at odds with her 'fidgetty' father, who was 'sometimes a little difficult'.[29] Left behind by Bertram, she found herself friendless – unsupported and painfully outnumbered. The only outlets for her emotions were of her own devising: her painting, her journal and her pets. But Miss Carter's timetable prevented wholesale absorption in her art; the consolations of the journal were middling. Previously Bertram's presence had provided Beatrix with a degree of self-affirmation – what she described later as 'a mutual admiration society':[30] their shared enthusiasms were their joint bulwark against their parents. In his absence home life unbalanced. There were disagreements, tension, discord. Discussing earthquakes the following spring, she commented in her journal 'domestic ones are only too frequent'.[31] And her health continued to fluctuate, as it always would. She succumbed to mumps. A gumboil kept her in bed for a week.[32] Bilious attacks left her too weak to travel across London by Underground.[33] 'Seven sorts of medicine, including calomel, and no solid[s]' were used to treat an autumn chill.[34] She began to think of herself, with partial justification, as an invalid. As late as June 1897, she decided to avoid Queen Victoria's Diamond Jubilee procession: 'It is too hot. I shall stop at home and hang a large flag out of the window.'[35] Whether her parents were responsible for this attitude, or simply sought to manipulate it, is unclear. 'Her mother tried to keep her as a semi-invalid far too much,' remembered one of Beatrix's cousins.[36]

Her birthday in July inspired no surge of happy feelings, although brother and sister were reunited for the summer holidays. 'I have heard it called "sweet seventeen", no indeed, what a time we are, have been having, and shall have'.[37] Without descending to details, Beatrix makes her feelings clear enough. Past, present, future: all inspire the same despondency. And that 'we' surely suggests unhappiness ingrained at the very heart of the family. She had begun thinking about the story that became *The Tale of Little Pig Robinson*; unsurprisingly, she failed to complete it. As finished in 1930, 'the most peculiar adventures that ever happened to a pig' include escape from predictable domesticity to an island of abundance. Provided with everything he could possibly want to eat – Beatrix's version of porcine fulfilment – Robinson is 'not at all inclined to return to Stymouth'. It sounds like wishful thinking.

Bertram would describe his mother as 'the sort of woman who would have you pushed in a perambulator until you got out and said you would rather walk'.[38] Rupert and Helen Potter lacked purpose and, apparently, ambition beyond the most run-of-the-mill social aspirations, but they wanted neither force of will nor the instinct to control. At seventeen, Beatrix remained in her mother's eyes a child. Beatrix's protest was largely confined to the silent mutterings of her journal. It was only her sense of vocation – untested and unproven – that encouraged her to dispute her mother's view.

Her unhappiness came and went, powerful while it lasted. In its grip she described her life as a 'dark journey'. 'Odious fits of low spirits' spoilt everything; she had begun to dread the future.[39] She did not propose a solution, though always at the back of her mind was the prospect of extra time to devote to her painting. In the meantime she ricocheted between more or less serious ailments. Nervous strain contributed to her affliction, which emerges from her journal as neurasthenic – painful headaches, unusual tiredness, lassitude, irritability, and all with no identifiable cause beyond an ongoing emotional uncertainty. For the most part the journal does not attribute blame directly and, in fact, culpability was not straightforward. If Helen Potter erred in not involving Beatrix in decisions about her continuing education, Beatrix was equally immoveable in her *idée fixe* that her future was only concerned with painting. As her rigorous self-imposed apprenticeship as a naturalist proved, Beatrix was every bit as determined as either of her parents. She admitted that the cause of 'so many scrapes' at home was her 'self-will'.[40] Emotionally she was out of kilter with both Helen and Rupert. Distant from her mother's world of social niceties and unable to impersonate with any conviction her father's ideas of finesse, she imagined herself cumbrous and ungainly; 'I feel like a cow in a drawing room,' she wrote on 29 April 1884.[41] Racked by shyness, Beatrix lacked self-assurance. Like Mr Jackson the toad, in the pristine house belonging to Mrs Tittlemouse in the bank under the hedge, she struggled to make herself 'fit'.

Among her resources were the paintings she saw in the many exhibitions she visited with Rupert. At the *Winter Exhibition of Old Masters*, held in January 1883 at the Royal Academy, Beatrix had been struck by an allegorical figure of Faith by Reynolds. The painting of the figure's face impressed her powerfully: fixed in her memory, she held fast to it like a totem. *Faith* was proof of art's potency; it was also her incentive. By aspiring to *Faith*'s distinctive qualities, Beatrix would achieve her ambition to 'do something'. In the short term, the single-mindedness of her focus challenged her parents' plans. The fixity with which she clung to her pipe dream contributed little to Beatrix's sense of wellbeing.

Once art had been an emollient aspect of Potter family life: Beatrix appears to have found it increasingly contentious. Her journal documents Rupert's critical response to the paintings he saw, including, in June 1884, those in the collection of the Ashmolean Museum in Oxford. 'They were dreadful, certainly some of them, but I am sure he has not the least idea of the difficulty of painting a picture. He can draw very well, but he has hardly attempted water-colour, and never oil. A person in this state, with a correct eye, and good taste, and great experience of different painters, sees all the failures and not the difficulties.'[42] In November Rupert's disdain targeted Millet and Corot.[43] Unsure of herself, and perhaps on the lookout for grounds for dissent, Beatrix assumed unfairly that her father's criticism would be redoubled in assessing her own efforts. She had begun to withhold her opinions when they were together: 'when I go to a gallery, I always avoid mentioning defects out loud (to myself I say what I like), however plainly I see them'. Regretfully she was afraid of 'showing much of my attempts to him'.

Rupert does not appear to have equated Beatrix's desire to paint with his own passion for photography; he did not act as any sort of intermediary with Helen on Beatrix's behalf or show Beatrix particular understanding. Beatrix acknowledged that hers was an obsession: like all obsessions, it had its irrational side. 'It is all the same, drawing, painting, modelling, the irresistible desire to copy any beautiful object which strikes the eye. Why cannot one be content to look at it? I cannot rest, I must draw, however poor the result.'[44] Arguably the very 'irresistibility' of Beatrix's desire proved the legitimacy of her feelings, but there was no one to support this view. Disorientated and lonely, she found herself relying on art to hold at bay her demons. 'When I have had a bad time come over me it is a stronger desire than ever,' she noted.[45] And so her dissatisfaction set her on a downward spiral. The inability to paint as much as she wished made for 'bad times', which in turn demanded painting as respite. Even 'the sight of... wonderful pictures' in London galleries had begun to cast her down.[46]

Having encouraged her taste for drawing and painting since infancy, the Potters did not deny their daughter's claim to a vocation. They arranged a costly course of twelve lessons in oil painting with a Mrs A., recommended by the widow of former president of the Royal Academy, Sir Charles Eastlake. These supplemented the lessons in drawing and watercolour that Beatrix had received from Miss Cameron since 1878. In both cases, Beatrix was quick to find herself out of sympathy with her teacher. Her response was to regard the lessons as a means of increasing her technical proficiency. Beatrix admitted that 'technical difficulties can be taught'; the ability to see must be innate.[47] She held as tightly as possible to her own way of doing things. After two lessons with Mrs A., she was already fretful in her journal: 'It is a risky thing to copy, shall I catch it?' So acute was her anxiety that it kept her awake at night.

She cannot have been an easy pupil. She complained that 'it is tiresome, when you do get some lessons, to be taught in a way you dislike and to have to swallow your feelings out of considerations at home and there.'[48] By the end of 1884 her conviction was stronger than ever that practice, not lessons, would improve her painting. With fine equivocation, she wrote in her journal 'I hope it is not pride that makes me so stiff against teaching, but a bad or indifferent teacher is worse than none. It cannot be taught, nothing after perspective, anatomy and the mixing of paints with medium.'[49] She clung to a statement by Millais: 'It is surprising how much is to be learnt alone.'[50] She does not record how much of this she communicated to her parents, but the reader's sympathies are divided between parents and child. What cannot be doubted is Beatrix's confidence in her own vision.

It was not enough to make her happy. As Beatrix concluded of her lessons with Miss Cameron, 'If you and your master are determined to look at nature and art in two different directions you are sure to stick', and determination undoubtedly played its part in Beatrix's reaction to both her teachers.[51] Her overwhelming desire to paint and pursue her own course made her frequently disaffected; it impacted on the solid regularity of life at 2 Bolton Gardens. Looking back over the course of 1885 in her journal, Beatrix described it as comprised of 'much bitterness and a few peaceful summer days. Oh life, wearisome, disappointing, and yet in many shades so sweet',[52] a self-conscious assessment that nevertheless accurately captures facets of her experience in her late teens and early twenties. She added that she was 'terribly afraid of the future. Some fears will inevitably be fulfilled, and the rest is dark.'

Alone in the nursery, mostly without Bertram, and yet to achieve any measure of independence through painting, writing – or marriage – she anticipated only darkness. She would describe herself as living 'so much asleep and out of life that the old world of books is almost as tangible as the new world of the *times*'.[53] Within that lament were seeds of her escape. The Beatrix of her late teens did not yet aspire to become a children's author, but in 'the old world of books' her salvation lay.

In the end it was 'a five minutes wonder' that propelled Beatrix into print at the age of twenty-four and offered her, relatively young, grounds for hope despite her unconventional ambitions. Short-term exigency also played a part: in her own words 'a desire for coin to the amount of £6'.[54]

She and Bertram wanted to buy a printing machine: at sixteen pounds, it was six pounds too expensive. Their joint expedient of Beatrix creating a series of designs for Christmas and New Year cards was trialled on members of their family over Christmas 1889. After fleeting initial approbation all round (the 'five minutes wonder'), it was Rupert's brother-in-law, Sir Henry Roscoe, married to his sister Lucy, who suggested a publisher 'would snap at' Beatrix's hand-drawn designs. No practical advice, or any offer of help, bolstered kind words.

More than a month elapsed, then Beatrix set to work 'privately to prepare Six Designs', the undertaking a secret from her parents. Benjamin Bouncer was her model; her best ideas, she claimed, came to her in chapel. As in her later work, the watercolours purchased for six pounds by Hildesheimer & Faulkner by return of post on 14 May 1890 included upright rabbit figures dressed in human clothes. Their hybrid costumes nodded to the eighteenth century: greatcoats, ribbons and dainty reticules. Hildesheimer & Faulkner afterwards issued Beatrix's designs as illustrations to a booklet of doggerel, *A Happy Pair*, by Frederick E. Weatherly, author of the popular song 'Roses of Picardy'. Her name did not appear in the booklet – only her initials, H. B. P.

Neither Miss Cameron nor Mrs A. had altered Beatrix's estimation of her own work. Nor did her meeting with Mr Faulkner, in his offices in the City, encourage Beatrix to reappraise the work she meant to undertake. 'He did not strike me as being a person with much taste,' she commented drily. She was happy with the deal she had struck: nothing in her own account suggests a temptation to compromise in order to perpetuate the association of Hildesheimer & Faulkner and H. B. P. The former wanted humour, anthropomorphism close to caricature. As time would show, Beatrix's own humour was subtler and more subversive. Her sole concession was the pair of drawings she offered Mr Faulkner of guinea pigs wearing trousers.[55]

Instead, over the course of the following year, she sent watercolours to Frederick Warne & Co. Founded in 1865, the company had already published illustrated books by Walter Crane and Kate Greenaway; in 1871 it issued Edward Lear's *Nonsense Songs, Stories, Botany* and *Alphabets*, which included Beatrix's favourite 'The Owl and the Pussy Cat'. Warne returned Beatrix sketches. On 12 November 1891, the company indicated that, in place of booklets, it would be happy to consider 'ideas & drawings in book form'.[56] A decade would pass before Beatrix rose to the challenge.

· 5 ·

'I shall tell you a story'

Beatrix with Benjamin H. Bouncer on a lead, September 1891. Known as Bounce, this rabbit was Beatrix's model for the first paintings she sold – to a greetings card publisher, Hildesheimer & Faulkner.

'I wish to hatch my own eggs; I will
hatch them all by myself'

The Tale of Jemima Puddle-Duck, 1908

I T BEGAN with an illness and a letter.

'I don't know what to write to you, so I shall tell you
a story about four little rabbits whose names were Flopsy,
Mopsy, Cottontail and Peter,' Beatrix wrote on 4 September
1893. She was in Perthshire with her parents. As she wrote,
she illustrated each of the eight pages. On the following
day she wrote again. 'Once upon a time there was a frog
called Mr Jeremy Fisher, and he lived in a little house on
the bank of a river.'

The first letter's recipient was Noel Moore, the eldest of
the children of Beatrix's former governess Annie Carter;
Beatrix addressed the second letter to Noel's brother Eric.
Like Beatrix as a child, Noel was often unwell. He was ill
in bed as she wrote, though not, as Beatrix explained of
Peter in her letter, 'in consequence of overeating himself'.[1]
Beatrix described him later as 'the lame boy', on account

103

of polio.[2] Fair-mindedness prompted the dispatch of Eric's letter, which she also illustrated.

Beatrix was a regular visitor to the Moores; she wrote to both boys over the course of the next decade. The habit had begun the previous spring, when she sent four-year-old Noel a letter from Falmouth: she illustrated her descriptions with doodles of palm trees and fishermen, chickens, ducks and a tabby cat on the harbour steps. On another occasion she was moved to write 'picture letters to the little Moores' from Scotland, watching 'a squirrel in the laburnum under the window mobbed by about thirty sparrows and some chaffinches'. 'Its fierce excited little movements,' she commented, 'reminded me of a monkey.'[3] With her on her visits to south London at one time and another she had taken Benjamin Bouncer and a succession of mice in their travelling boxes. These and other animals populated the letters Beatrix sent Noel, Eric and, in time, their sisters Freda, Marjorie, Norah, Joan and Hilda; Beatrix sent no picture letters to the youngest Moore daughter, her goddaughter and namesake Beatrix. Without news to share, she took refuge in storytelling – in addition to Peter Rabbit and Jeremy Fisher, ideas that would become the tales of Pig Robinson and Squirrel Nutkin and chapters of *The Fairy Caravan*.

Beatrix was twenty-seven, unmarried and childless when she described to Noel those 'four little rabbits'. At the end of her life, she would assert that 'the secret of good writing is to have something to say – and write with an end in view';[4] she advised an aspiring writer to write as if for her own children, as she had directed her story purposefully at a particular child. In September 1893, Beatrix's end in writing to Noel Moore her first version of *The Tale of Peter Rabbit* was Noel's distraction: as she commented afterwards, 'Peter never aspired to be high art.'[5] Nor, with the letter posted, did her own thoughts dwell on her story. Unsurprisingly, she set Peter's tale in 'that pleasant unchanging world of realism and romance' which meant for Beatrix the countryside, a region where fact and fancy could profitably overlap.[6] Her journal is unrevealing about the Scottish holiday that year or her state of mind: there is nothing to suggest that Beatrix intended more for either Noel or Eric's stories than the boys' immediate entertainment.

Yet she approached each letter as she would her finished tales. She wrote with economy and humour, closely matching her pen-and-ink illustrations to events described. Several of Beatrix's pictures in Noel's letter were recycled virtually unaltered in the published tale: Mrs Rabbit dosing Peter with camomile tea, Peter encountering Mr McGregor round the end of the cucumber frame. Beatrix used Benjamin for her model; her drawings are without backgrounds and all botanical details are simplified, but there is evidence of that 'thoroughness' on which she prided herself – in the sureness of her draughtsman-ship and Peter's tangible emotions so simply conveyed. 'Children take things seriously,' Beatrix wrote.[7] Her own seriousness of purpose matched childish earnestness. Noel Moore's story represents the epistolary equivalent of a dress rehearsal – albeit the interval between Beatrix's letter and publication in book form was lengthy.

Aged nineteen, Beatrix had been critical in her apprais-al of a drawing by John Flaxman, whom she otherwise admired. Flaxman's subject in this instance was a Cyclops, one of the mythical race of one-eyed giants. Beatrix con-sidered it a failure. Searching for an explanation, she told herself that drawing that was wholly imaginary could never succeed. 'There is no such thing as imagination, in the vulgar sense of forming what never has been seen, it is all patchwork and imitation. Having seen eyes, it is easy enough to say "having one eye instead of two", but it is impossible to tell what the creature would look like.'[8] It was not a trap into which she meant to fall. From childhood her drawing had focused on accurate observation. Once she began writing for children, the same impulse – towards 'patchwork and imitation' – marked her illustrations, start-ing with her letter to Noel Moore: Peter is a real rabbit; the setting for his adventure is an amalgam of gardens Beatrix knew; within this garden the reader recognises broad beans, lettuces and cabbage, a gooseberry net and a basket exactly large enough to trap a wild rabbit (this will eventually become a circular sieve). When Beatrix came to draw Jeremy Fisher the next day, she was able to take inspiration from her memories of her own frog, Punch, supplemented by black-and-white illustrations to *A Frog He Would A-Wooing Go* by Randolph Caldecott: four of Caldecott's frog sketches, bought by Rupert, hung in Bolton Gardens, visible whenever Beatrix was at home. She had no need to rely on 'imagination in the vulgar sense'.

In her sketchbooks she had practised accurately recording nature; in the nursery, training a mouse with a handkerchief or teaching her hedgehog to drink milk from a cup, she had imbued nature with human personality, blurring distinctions between animal and human in the fashion of writers from Aesop to Joel Chandler Harris, author of the 'Brer Rabbit' stories, both of whom she read and enjoyed. She read fairy tales, nursery rhymes and old collections of children's verse; in Scotland the following year she spent a hot afternoon reading *Rhymes and Fairy Tales* by Robert Chambers, author of *Popular Rhymes of Scotland* and *Poems for Young People*.[9] Hand in hand with her inclination towards anthropomorphism was a narrative dimension to Beatrix's pictures – the reason Hildesheimer & Faulkner were able to reuse her designs for Christmas cards to illustrate Weatherly's doggerel. Truncated and uncoloured, the version of the Peter Rabbit story Beatrix sent Noel Moore was still capable of capturing a child's imagination. Intrinsic to its success was the deftness of her sketches, described by Beatrix as 'scribbled pen and ink', and the sharpness of her focus: stories written for 'real children'.[10]

Throughout the 1890s, Beatrix worked on illustrations. The undertaking offered diversion from the yawning, empty hours and possibility of payment. *A Frog he would a-fishing go*, another of her Caldecott-influenced variants on the Jeremy Fisher story, was published by Ernest Nister; the same company also published what Beatrix described as a cat drawing with 'a shop background'.[11] Two sequences of illustrations to rhymes using mice as models – 'There was an old woman who lived in a shoe' and 'Three little mice sat down to spin' – failed to find publishers to turn them into booklets along the lines of *A Happy Pair*. (Instead, an illustration from the former provided the template for Hunca Munca and her babies in *The Tale of Two Bad Mice*; Beatrix reprised one of her 'Three little mice' sketches in *The Tailor of Gloucester*. She was thrifty with her work and set a high value on her creativity.)

Beatrix illustrated scenes from Uncle Remus stories, from *Alice's Adventures in Wonderland* and 'Cinderella'. Consistently avoiding 'forming what has never been seen', in each case she used Peter as her model – for Carroll's Knave of Hearts, a white rabbit complete with tabard and ruff, and for the team of six rabbits in harness, who draw through moonlit streets Cinderella's pumpkin coach.

In *The Tale of Mr Tod*, a footpath winds slowly up a wooded slope. Wood sorrel and moss fringe its course. In a thicket where trees have been cleared are 'leafy oak stumps, and a sea of blue hyacinths'. In *The Fairy Caravan*, Pringle Wood is 'almost silent, almost still; save for a whispering breath amongst the golden green leaves, and a faint tingle ringle from the bluebells on the fairy hill of oaks... beneath the trees, wave upon wave, a blue sea of bluebells'.

Beatrix loved woodland, 'rich land, scattered clumps of fine timber and a fringe of natural wood'.[12] As a child, she witnessed the felling of the last walnut trees in Kensington: the disappearance of a rural past. Among her disappointments on revisiting Dalguise was the loss of the ancient plum tree in the garden. A story letter she wrote in 1916 described consequences of tree felling: a tree fairy without a home, its lifeline severed. She incorporated a version of this story in *The Fairy Caravan*: 'Surely it is cruel to cut down a very fine tree!' Her fondness encompassed fantasy: for Beatrix, woods were liminal areas, the margin where reality and unreality merged. She claimed that fir woods in the Lake District 'recall[ed] one's childish fancies of wolves, a very striking background they would make for Grimm's Fairy Tales'.[13]

Woodland provided habitat for many of the animals she wrote about. At ground level it was also home to fungi. For a decade, fungi occupied many of Beatrix's thoughts, her intense engagement far outstripping her apparently light-hearted creation of first versions of her stories of Peter Rabbit and Jeremy Fisher. As with woodland, her engagement had an imaginative aspect – sometimes to the point of whimsy. She remembered sitting on Oatmeal Crag, near Esthwaite, 'and all the little tiny fungus people singing and bobbing and dancing in the grass and under the leaves all down below... and I sitting above and knowing something about them. I cannot tell what possesses me with the fancy that they laugh and clap their hands... I suppose it is the fairy rings, the myriads of fairy fungi that start into life in autumn woods.'[14] At other times the excitement of mycology was artistic or scientific. Of all Beatrix's natural history interests, her study of the 'forty thousand named and classified funguses' came closest to compulsion.[15]

Her wholehearted absorption provided Beatrix with oc-cupation, typically during the second half of long family holidays, when the weather and time of year combined to carpet the Highlands and the Lakes with specimens. Legitimately, Beatrix could spend time apart from her parents engaged in her search, driving herself in a carriage and pony to likely spots; the solitariness of her pursuit was itself a recommendation. As she commented in her jour-nal, summing up the family's Scottish holiday in 1894, 'it is somewhat trying to pass a season of enjoyment in the company of persons who are constantly on the outlook for matters of complaint';[16] she had no need to identify those 'persons'. In addition, mycology provided distraction at a time when Beatrix continued to feel isolated and dis-contented, particularly following the death in 1891 of her adored grandmother, Jessy Potter. Jessy's death at the age of ninety resulted in the sale of Camfield Place. Another part of Beatrix's childhood was consigned to memory. She asked for – and was given – bedroom furniture from Camfield: 'the bed with green damask curtains... because the green curtains were full of pretty dreams'.[17] Thirty years later, she used it in one of her last illustrations, 'Louisa Pussy-cat Sleeps Late', in *The Fairy Caravan*.

She found her first fungus specimens in the Lake District, at Lingholm in 1887. Camfield Place (until its sale),

Putney Park and woods in Berwickshire and Perthshire also proved fertile hunting grounds; she combed the rubbish heap at Wray Castle and, in Coldstream, with her customary lack of squeamishness, she spotted 'a *Cortinarius*, brittle and graceful on bleached horse-dung in [a] bog'.[18] From the beginning, the process of discovery contributed an excitement that never abated. She was lucky in encountering rarities: fungi 'like a spluttered candle', 'one with white spikes on the lower side' and, in March 1897, a 'little fungus like red holly berries, it had only been found once before in Scotland'.[19] On 18 August 1894, with something approaching salivation, she described her discovery of 'an ideal heavenly dream of the toadstool eaters'; the setting was the wood near Hatchednize, in Coldstream.[20]

As formerly with plants and insects, and like her passion for fossils, her interest lay in the patient, precise recording of as many varieties as possible, and she painted and photographed her finds. Hatchednize Wood did not disappoint; successful identification added to her pleasure. 'The fungus starred the ground apparently in thousands, a dozen sorts in sight at once, and such specimens... I found upwards of twenty sorts in a few minutes, *Cortinarius* and the handsome *Lactarius deliciosus* being conspicuous and, joy of joys, the spiky *Gomphidius glutinosus*, a round, slimy, purple head among the moss, which I took up carefully with my old cheese-knife, and turning over saw the slimy veil.' Lingeringly she inventoried the treasure trove in her journal. She described her capture of *Gomphidius glutinosus* with the sensual relish of a sexual encounter. Breathless, she revelled in each lubricious detail: colour, texture, fragility. Two years later, the memory remained fresh: 'One has a pleasant sensation sometimes. I remember so well finding *Gomphidius glutinosus*.'[21] In Hatchednize Wood Beatrix stepped into a private fairy tale, her 'ideal heavenly dream'. She had '[found] a totally new species for the first time'; it inspired feelings of 'extreme complacency'.[22] Here was the satisfaction whose absence she so often bewailed. She painted *Gomphidius glutinosus* amid the moss and low growth of the woodland floor, the sheen of its slimy cap and the gills beneath the cap: an image as minutely detailed as any early work by Millais. It was one of 'about 40 careful drawings of fungi' she completed that summer. Other subjects included the fairy ring fungus, *Marasmius oreades*.[23] Observing the state of crops in surrounding fields, she asked 'how without the aid of the fairy-folk... could there be so little mildew in the corn?'[24]

Her interest in fungi would bring Beatrix happiness but, ultimately, frustration. In the short term she was fortunate to find a fellow enthusiast. Until his retirement, Charles McIntosh had been the rural postman at Dalguise, 'a scared startled scarecrow... very tall and thin, stooping with a weak chest, a long wisp of whisker blowing over either shoulder, a drip from his hat and his nose', a 'painfully shy' man who, despite none of Beatrix's advantages of background, had made himself a recognised authority on British fungi.[25] A member of the Cryptogamic Society of Scotland (dedicated since 1875 to the study of lichen, mosses, ferns, algae and fungi), he discovered thirteen new fungus species; botanical notes by McIntosh were used by Francis Buchanan White in compiling *The Flora of Perthshire* in 1898. For as long as Beatrix could remember, the sight of Charles McIntosh on his fifteen-mile daily round, undertaken on foot in all weathers, had been a feature of Potter family holidays.

In October 1892, Beatrix was staying with her parents in Birnam, on the opposite bank of the Tay from Dunkeld; Bertram had lately travelled south for his first term at Oxford. At the end of the month, after 'trying all summer', she spoke to Charles McIntosh at last. (She had overcome their mutual shyness as well as the social restrictions that impeded an unmarried young woman approaching an unmarried man of different class.) The meeting was a success. Beatrix showed McIntosh her drawings; McIntosh 'became quite excited and spoke with quite poetical feelings about [fungi's] exquisite colours'.[26] He promised to post specimens to her in London, and did so.

Beatrix repaid his kindness by sending him copies of her fungus paintings. In her letters she refers to herself in the third person as 'Miss Potter', a formality that underlined the gulf between them. McIntosh replied in kind to 'Miss Potter, Madam'. But he also offered guidance and advice, notably that her drawings include 'separate sketches of sections' of a given specimen.[27] Beatrix consulted McIntosh over identification and, once, concerning the 'curious' emergence of a pale yellow, hundred-'fingered' fungus on a piece of broom 'put away in a tin canister & forgotten... in a hot cupboard near the kitchen chimny [sic]'.[28] Specialist publications in Rupert Potter's library made few concessions to the layman; to Beatrix's considerable frustration, the staff of the Natural History Museum '[took] no interest whatever in funguses at large'.[29] In her letters McIntosh became her sounding board and her authority. The description of their meeting in Beatrix's journal suggests condescension on Beatrix's part: in her letters they are equals, conspirators who share an obsession.

The Potters returned to Perthshire the following summer. Rupert took a large house in Dunkeld, called Eastwood. Beatrix and Charles McIntosh resumed their collaboration. In the Eastwood garden Beatrix unearthed another rarity, *Stribolomyces strobilaceus*; naturally she painted it. It did not occupy her thoughts exclusively.

Fossils continued to fascinate her: with their monochrome colouring, they too posed specific challenges for
the watercolourist. The day after she painted *Stribolomyces
stribolaceus* she wrote to Noel Moore about 'four little rabbits'; the next day she invented a story about a fishing
frog. Her rabbit letter included a Scottish gardener called
McGregor. Beatrix disclaimed the existence of a model for
Peter's tormentor. With his long, thin face and straggling
beard, and the suggestion of a 'broken lamppost' in his
gangling gait, he resembled Charles McIntosh.

On the third floor at Bolton Gardens, Beatrix germinated
fungi – eventually as many as forty to fifty different kinds of
spore, according to a letter she wrote to Charles McIntosh
in February 1897. Her purpose is unclear. Within days of
this letter, she wrote to Walter Gaddum, nine-year-old son
of her cousin Edith Potter, 'I have been drawing funguses
very hard, I think some day they will be put in a book but it
will be a dull one to read.'[30] Her interest was simultaneously
scientific and artistic. To McIntosh she described what was
clearly botanical research; to Walter, she indicated that her
goal was botanical illustration. At what stage, or indeed
why, the balance of her interest tipped from the painterly
to the scientific is not certain. The mechanics of nature had

always engrossed her. That she should steep herself in 'curious work with fungus spore', trying to unravel a theory, at the same time as transforming her specimens as accurately as possible into works of art, is not out of character.[31] Again Beatrix's approach was 'painstaking' and 'thorough'.

In May 1896, Beatrix had met the director and assistant director of the Royal Botanic Gardens at Kew, William Thiselton-Dyer and George Massee. She owed her introductions to her uncle, Sir Henry Roscoe. Vice-chancellor of the University of London and a former Liberal MP, Roscoe was also a distinguished chemist. For his work in inorganic chemistry, especially photochemistry, he had won considerable acclaim; his *Spectrum Analysis* of 1869 ran to multiple editions. At Christmas 1889, it was Roscoe who had encouraged Beatrix to find a publisher for her Christmas card designs.

If such an offhand commendation amounts to championing his niece, it is possible that Roscoe had recognised something uncongenial to Beatrix in the atmosphere at 2 Bolton Gardens during the difficult decade of her twenties. He may have been impressed by the rigour of her study or simply have shared the fascination of his shy and otherworldly niece with the complex processes of fungus reproduction; Beatrix did her part to fuel his interest, even writing to him secretly from the family holiday in the autumn of 1896. Either way, it was apparently Roscoe, the professional scientist, who gave fuel to Beatrix's fixation by encouraging her to collate and order her findings in the form of a research paper. To that end, he facilitated two interviews with Thiselton-Dyer at Kew, and, through the latter, a reader's card for Beatrix to the Kew libraries to assist her in her studies.

The story of Beatrix Potter's thwarting by the authorities at Kew Gardens has been told before. It was indeed the case that Beatrix, busy with microscope and slides in the nursery at Bolton Gardens, uncovered aspects of the process of fungus germination by spores, and that her discoveries appeared to challenge work in progress by George Massee at Kew. With naïve heavy-handedness Beatrix assured Thiselton-Dyer that her work was groundbreaking and worthy of Kew's attention; she forecast that, with no one to validate her theories, German researchers would get there first and 'it would be in all the books in ten years'.[32] The Kew director did not rise to the bait. Instead, in their second interview he referred Beatrix to the Professor of Botany at Cambridge, Henry Marshall Ward, himself (unlike Thiselton-Dyer) a specialist mycologist. Correctly Beatrix interpreted the rebuff. She characterised Thiselton-Dyer as cynical and boastful, 'a short-tempered, clever man with a very good opinion of his Establishment, and jealous of outsiders'; she described his manner of address as 'on the outside edge of civil'.[33] Her opinion was apparently justified by the letter discussing her proposals that he subsequently sent her uncle. Roscoe considered it *rude* and *stupid* and concealed its contents from Beatrix. Beatrix accurately guessed its bent. Her assessment of Thiselton-Dyer as a martinet – and misogynistic to boot – was close to the mark.

Afterwards Beatrix stated that it was Roscoe's annoyance 'at the slighting of anything under his patronage' and his 'animosity against the authorities at Kew' that had influenced his determination that her paper be read to the Linnean Society in order to gain the acknowledgement he had decided it merited; the impulse was not her own and her journal contains no indication that she sought either the society's endorsement or its acclaim.[34] Nevertheless, it was Kew's George Massee – more willing to countenance Beatrix's theories than Thiselton-Dyer – who, on 1 April 1897, presented her paper, 'On the Germination of the Spores of Agaricineae', to members at Burlington House (as a woman Beatrix was ineligible for Linnean Society membership and barred from meetings). Massee told Beatrix its reception had been positive, but that the society felt the paper needed further work. It seems unlikely that Beatrix's paper, the work of a female amateur, was ever seriously considered. No copy of it survives. That summer, again on holiday in the Lake District, Beatrix completed additional fungus paintings, including an image of the startling scarlet waxcap, *Hygrocybe coccinea*. Unlike the lost paper, she took particular care of them for the rest of her life.

Eight years separate Beatrix's story letter to Noel Moore from publication of a privately printed edition of *The Tale of Peter Rabbit* on 16 December 1901.

If the intervention of Sir Henry Roscoe failed to benefit Beatrix's mycological studies, the encouragement of Annie Moore, who first suggested Beatrix turn her story into a book, and the assistance of Hardwicke Rawnsley, who redoubled that encouragement, proved more fruitful in her search for a publisher.

Rawnsley was rector of the church of St Margaret of Antioch, Wray-on-Windermere. A mercurial temperament and wide-ranging interests earned for him the epithet 'the most active volcano in Europe'. The founder of the Lake District Defence Society and the Keswick School of Industrial Arts – the latter intended 'to counteract the pernicious effect of turning men into machines without possibility of love of their work' – he campaigned over a number of years for what, in 1895, became the National

Trust for Places of Historic Interest or Natural Beauty; Rawnsley acted as honorary secretary until his death in 1920.[35] So extensive were his commitments, including his position on Cumberland county council and as a canon of Carlisle Cathedral, that, in 1898, he was forced to decline promotion to the bishopric of Madagascar. Instead he protested tirelessly against bugbears that included white bread, slot machines on station platforms and saucy seaside postcards. Somehow he found time to write more than forty books, many on Lake District subjects, and prodigious quantities of poetry. His *Ballads of Brave Deeds* of 1896, inspired by 'reverential admiration for affecting and splendid self-sacrifice', was followed, in 1897, by the popular *Moral Rhymes for the Young*.[36]

Energetic and sociable, Rawnsley visited the Potters at Wray Castle in the summer of 1882. This vigorous dynamo in his early thirties, stocky in build, with startlingly blue eyes, ought to have overwhelmed the cripplingly shy sixteen-year-old Beatrix. Instead, engaged in inventorying the excavation of a nearby Roman villa, he talked to her about archaeology and geology. A former student of Ruskin and friend of painter G. F. Watts, he encouraged her in her drawing. According to Rawnsley family legend, he fell a little in love with Beatrix.

With Rupert Potter Hardwicke Rawnsley shared his

121

interest in Wordsworth, photography and conservation; Rawnsley subsequently lay behind Rupert's life member-ship of the National Trust. Although the Potters later based themselves elsewhere in the Lake District – in houses at Ambleside, Windermere, Keswick and Sawrey – Rawnsley's appointment in 1883 as vicar of Crosthwaite and rural dean of Keswick, where he remained until retirement in 1917, afforded him ongoing, if sporadic, contact. As a success-ful children's poet, he was an obvious choice for Beatrix to consult in 1901 following Annie Moore's suggestion of publishing her picture letter as a full-length story.

Rawnsley made a number of recommendations; Bertram also offered suggestions. To each in turn Beatrix dispatched the manuscript she temporarily entitled 'The Tale of Peter Rabbit and Mr McGregor's Garden'. 'The original Peter went all round the town before he found a publisher,' she wrote: every response disappointed and she apologised to the Moore children for keeping their picture letters so long.[37] Four years previously, she had weathered the combined indifference of Thiselton-Dyer and the Linnean Society, ultimately with something like equanimity. Now, rejection by publishers provoked a degree of obduracy. With the same impatience of obstacles she had outlined fifteen years ear-lier in her journal concerning her need to paint, Beatrix set about publishing the book herself.

Like Jemima Puddle-duck intent on hatching her eggs –
'I wish to hatch my own eggs; I will hatch them all by
myself' – Beatrix in her early thirties had become determined one way or another to see her story in print in her
own preferred format: 'a booklet 5 x 3¾ inches, on rather
rough stout paper', illustrated in black and white in order
to avoid 'the great expense of colour printing – and also the
rather uninteresting colour of a good many of the subjects
which are most of them rabbit-brown and green'.[38] On personal recommendation she entrusted her commission to
Strangeways & Sons, of Tower Street, London. Illustrations
were engraved by the Art Reproduction Company of Fetter
Lane and a coloured frontispiece – the only colour picture
in the book – produced by Hentschel of Fleet Street. Beatrix
ordered 250 copies from Strangeways, and 500 frontis-
pieces in the event of a reprint. The undertaking proved
costly and tells us much of her confidence in the enterprise
and her single-mindedness.[39] Certainly this was the light in
which she herself regarded the venture: 'I think I may say
I have shown considerable spirit in bringing it out myself!'
she wrote.[40] She showed similar spirit in tenaciously selling
and distributing all 250 copies and ordering a reprint of a
further 200 copies. She recouped her costs, she indicated,
through sales to 'obliging aunts'; word of mouth evidently
played its part too.[41]

Among purchasers of the privately printed version of *The Tale of Peter Rabbit* was Arthur Conan Doyle, whose Sherlock Holmes stories had been turned down in 1886 by Frederick Warne & Co. With mingled pleasure and diffidence, on 19 January 1902 Beatrix reported Conan Doyle's 'good opinion of the story & words'.[42] It was a response that would become, as it remains, all but universal. By then it was also the opinion of Frederick Warne & Co.

Ten years previously, in the gentlest of rejections, Warne's had outlined to Beatrix possible interest in an illustrated book. Rawnsley rekindled their lukewarm favour. He informed them of Beatrix's arrangement with Strangeways & Sons and offered them a version of the Peter Rabbit story rewritten in cloying doggerel of his own. This time, at last, the publishers bit. Declining the clergyman's versifying, in September 1901 Frederick Warne & Co. resumed a correspondence with Beatrix Potter that would continue for the remainder of her life.

· 6 ·

'All the beasts can talk'

Shy but self-contained, Beatrix at twenty-six, photographed
at Birnam in Scotland.

'Duchess was quite delighted
with her own cleverness!'

The Tale of the Pie and the Patty-Pan, 1905

A S LONG AS she remained under her parents' roof,
Beatrix led a sheltered life. Rupert and Helen Potter's
stifling parenting ensured that their daughter's experiences
outside the family circle were virtually non-existent. In the
wake of her cousin Kate's mésalliance in 1885, Beatrix had
appraised Rupert's social connections: 'If he had a beautiful
daughter like Kate there is no doubt he could marry her
very well.' She pointed to her father's intimacy with 'rich
and respectable Unitarians' and even 'fashionable society'.[1]
But time passed and Rupert failed to find a suitor for his
own daughter.

It may not have been Rupert's fault. Without apparent
regret Beatrix noted of the party her parents hosted within
weeks of her nineteenth birthday, 'Cupid unavoidably
absent.' She had most enjoyed talking to her great-uncle,
Thomas Ashton, who reminded her of Grandmother

Leech.[2] Notwithstanding her own verdict that she had acquitted herself surprisingly well (considering her gaucherie and farouche dislike of company), it was an evening on which the Potters' likely exasperation seems forgiveable. Parties are not subsequently a feature of Beatrix's journal and it may be that her parents simply gave up.

If this were the case, Rupert and Helen replaced one conventional aspiration with another. Like other unmarried daughters, Beatrix was expected to take her place at her mother's side running 2 Bolton Gardens and overseeing the Potters' frequent travel arrangements. It was a shackle of sorts and she would refer to 'muddles here with servants which make me rather tied'.[3] Beatrix's journal gives ample evidence of her unsuitedness to this role of 'angel in the house', the mid-Victorian stereotype of women as docile domestic paragons revelling in their own submission. Neither Rupert nor Helen was privy to Beatrix's journal; neither fully conceived her strength of will, the extent of her determination to 'do something' or achieve some measure of independence. Both were aims contrary to the self-effacement and humility expected of the stay-at-home daughter.

Beatrix accepted domestic incarceration with an ill will but few overt signs of protest. During an illness of her mother's in 1895, she snapped, 'There is supposed to be some angelic sentiment in tending the sick, but personally I should not associate angels with castor oil and empty-ing slops', a statement convincingly out of kilter with the Victorian paradigm.[4] She did her duty nevertheless. Beatrix's misfortune lay in her parents' lack of imagin-ation and the prescriptiveness of contemporary practice. Having 'failed' to get married, she found herself lacking any third option. Her choices were circumscribed by parental expectation and by powerful social pressures in favour of conformity. Like others of her generation, she had never known anything else. In the main her parents' behaviour was conditioned by habit rather than malignity. Beatrix did not challenge the legitimacy of these assumptions, only their implications. And perhaps what chiefly motivated Rupert and Helen Potter was a determination to control. Key to maintaining the uneventfulness of their prosperous lives was an exaggerated focus on orderliness.

At the age of nineteen, Beatrix was unfamiliar even with the topography of London, as wholly a stranger to much of the capital as Timmy Willie, 'who had lived all his life in a garden'. Of a trip to the theatre with her parents and cousin Emily Potter in March 1885, Beatrix concluded, after a traf-fic jam in Buckingham Palace Road, that 'the drive there was the most interesting part of the affair': she admired the 'grand carriages' lined up outside Buckingham Palace and, at the end of the evening, Beefeaters marching. Although she had been born in London, 'extraordinary to state, it was the first time in my life that I had been past the Horse Guards, Admiralty, and Whitehall, or seen the Strand and the Monument'.[5]

When her black moods lifted, domestic adversity provided grist for Beatrix's humour. In the summer of 1894, she went to stay in the Cotswolds with her cousin Caroline Hutton. Beatrix was almost twenty-eight: she reported that she 'had not been away independently for five years'. With a degree of wryness she referred to the trip as 'an event'.[6] She indicated the stratagems attempted by her parents to dissuade her – 'It was so much of an event in the eyes of my relations that they made it appear an undertaking to me' – hinting at both cynicism and calculation in their arguments. 'I began to think I would rather not go. I had a sick headache most inopportunely, though whether cause or effect I could not say.'[7] Only the intervention of forceful cousin Caroline, five years Beatrix's junior, carried the day. Together – and without mishap – the young women made the journey by rail from Paddington to Stroud.

There were to be lasting effects of Beatrix's visit to the Huttons. Caroline Hutton appeared to Beatrix as a revelation. Beatrix described her as 'a pickle', always for her a term of fondness, and likened her to Jane Austen's Emma;

she marvelled at her physical prowess – her 'longish firm steps' as she strode across the country 'like a soldier who has been drilled' – and an unabashed quality in her character: her self-possession, fearlessness, decision. Both physical and mental attributes distinguished the young women. Weeks after this visit, Beatrix mistook her twenty-eighth birthday for her twenty-ninth: the confusion indicates more than absentmindedness. 'A good deal of geology and Shakespeare might be stuffed into the extra year,' she reassured herself limply.[8] It does not suggest a high value placed on her vanishing youth or self-possession.

By contrast Beatrix wrote of Caroline, 'the prevailing impression was of freshness and extreme amusement'.[9] Alert to her cousin's shortcomings, and with no desire to emulate what she considered her 'complete absence of imagination', nonetheless Beatrix recognised in Caroline Hutton a kindred spirit and a wake-up call: her impressions of her would act as a stiffener to Beatrix's own resolve. She considered her 'clever, brilliantly attractive and perfectly well principled, although knowing her own mind', a description which, barring physical appearances, applied equally to herself.[10] The regime at Bolton Gardens sought to deny scope for Beatrix's cleverness and principles; neither Rupert nor Helen encouraged their daughter to know her own mind. Her role as prop and amanuensis did not require self-knowledge, much less self-will.

This was not a revelation in the summer of 1894. In essentials Beatrix's life had changed little since 1883, the replacement of Miss Hammond by Miss Carter and the latter's subsequent departure. As a grown-up daughter Beatrix lived a double life: her parents' child, attentive against a backdrop of aspidistras and querulous respectability; and an independent-minded young woman of singular talents but few outlets. Her visit to the Huttons ahead of the family holiday to Berwickshire highlighted the absences and inconsistencies in Beatrix's life. Caroline's 'old-fashioned wisdom and... unreasoning fearlessness' upbraided Beatrix's own timidity. The cousins sat up into the night. In her dressing gown, with hair tumbled about her ears and 'her honest grey eyes round in the candle light', Caroline became 'all in a splutter', happily disputatious about religion, metaphysics and the insanitary living conditions of agricultural labourers. The women talked about love: Beatrix referred to 'an analytical discussion of the passions'; Caroline was vigorous in disclaiming any desire to be married.[11] It was the sort of cosy, affectionate, exploratory chatter from which her parents had largely barred Beatrix; it also points to an emotional curiosity on Beatrix's part of which her parents may have been unaware. Little wonder that she remembered aspects of her visit as 'like a most pleasant dream'.[12] It differed substantially from the 'prosperous uneventful' routines of Bolton Gardens.

In Beatrix's tales, examples of supportive female friendships are few. Ribby patronises Tabitha Twitchit in *The Tale of Samuel Whiskers*. In *The Tale of the Pie and the Patty-Pan*, Duchess mistrusts Ribby. The prospect of a party for her 'friends', in *The Tale of Tom Kitten*, throws Tabitha Twitchit into confusion. In *The Tale of Two Bad Mice*, the dolls Lucinda and Jane are separated by class, as well as being physically unable to speak to one another. Rebeccah Puddle-duck takes no interest in her sister-in-law Jemima's longing for ducklings in *The Tale of Jemima Puddle-Duck*: at best her attitude is dismissive. Instead, it is children – not adults or parents – who, in Beatrix's fictional world, are more often capable of companionship: Peter Rabbit and Benjamin Bunny; Flopsy, Mopsy and Cottontail; Tom Kitten, Moppet and Mittens; Pigling Bland and Pigwig. None resorts to dissembling; all appear impervious to hierarchy. The emphasis, as in much of Beatrix's life, is on siblings and cousins.

Beatrix's visit to the Huttons at Harescombe Grange took place nine months after her Peter Rabbit and Jeremy Fisher letters to the Moores. Beatrix does not record whether she discussed with her cousin the embryonic stories she had written the previous autumn and there is no reason to assume she did. In the early summer of 1894, she had yet to settle on children's books as her chief creative outlet; her interests in fungi and fossils were every bit as strong. So was her absorption in illustrating favourite stories and books, each of them more painstaking and time-consuming than the rapid pen-and-ink sketches of Noel and Eric's letters. Beatrix and Caroline had soon arrived at a state of rewarding intimacy. Beatrix's dismissal of her cousin as unimaginative may point to a lack of interest on Caroline's part in Beatrix's anthropomorphic fantasies or simply an assumption by Beatrix about Caroline's likely response. In Beatrix's account, there is an unliterary bent to Caroline's conversation.

Nevertheless, lack of imagination did not prevent Caroline Hutton from sharing with Beatrix a story the latter chose to regard in the light of a real-life fairy tale. It concerned a tailor in nearby Gloucester. John Prichard had left a suit of clothes unfinished at the end of the week. After a weekend's absence, he found it completed bar a single buttonhole – inexplicably and as if by magic, even down to a note: 'No more twist'. Cannily he exploited the story for promotional purposes. It acquired the status of local legend: Caroline heard it 'from Miss Lucy of Gloucester, who had it of the tailor'.[13] From first telling it made a

Foxgloves are the subject of one of Beatrix's earliest surviving sketches, from February 1876. This watercolour, with a pencil sketch of a bird, dates from 1903.

At Melford Hall in Suffolk, the home of Beatrix's cousin Ethel, Lady Hyde Parker,
she worked on *The Tale of Squirrel Nutkin* and *The Tailor of Gloucester*.
At Christmas 1903, she painted this oak-panelled interior.

Beatrix painted *Amanitopsis vaginata* on 30 August 1897,
the last summer of her fascination with fungi.

After her purchase of Hill Top, Beatrix painted a number of Lake District views, many for her own pleasure including 'A view over hills and valleys', c. 1905–13.

'The Meal' is one of a set of four illustrations which Beatrix called 'The Rabbits' Christmas Party' and gave to her aunt, Lucy Roscoe.

Beatrix celebrated her lifelong love of old-fashioned rhymes in
Appley Dapply's Nursery Rhymes and *Cecily Parsley's Nursery Rhymes* –
as well as a selection of unpublished illustrations like this farmyard
scene of 1905 entitled 'Come dance a jig to my Granny's pig'

In her illustrations for *The Tailor of Gloucester*, her favourite of
the 'little books', Beatrix combined her love of old china and
historic textiles with her fondness for mice.

This sketch of water lilies on Esthwaite Water, painted in 1906, suggests backgrounds to *The Tale of Mr. Jeremy Fisher*, published the same year.

powerful impression on Beatrix. Transformed into *The Tailor of Gloucester*, it became her favourite of her books. She asked the Huttons to show her the tailor's shop and she sketched the city's old uneven streets.

Beatrix's rewriting of Prichard's story was of long gestation. She did not begin work on it until 1901, seven years after she first heard it, by which time plans for private publication of *The Tale of Peter Rabbit* were well advanced, and Beatrix's negotiations with Frederick Warne & Co. for commercial publication the following year were also nearing completion. Like her Peter Rabbit story, Beatrix first addressed *The Tailor of Gloucester* to a child – a Christmas present, in December 1901, for Winifred Moore, known as Freda, the second of Noel and Eric's six sisters.

On this occasion, Beatrix did not choose a letter as the medium for her storytelling. In a stiff-covered exercise book, complete with watercolour illustrations and tied with pink ribbons, she unravelled a wholly personal interpretation of Caroline's quaint tale. Mice, Beatrix's favourite animals, became the magic agents; a cat called Simpkin suggested a malign Puss-in-Boots. As in *The Tale of Peter Rabbit*, in the finished story 'all the beasts can talk', though, as Beatrix explained, 'there are very few folk that can hear them, or know what it is that they say.' As in all her books, her own role was that of intermediary between beasts and folk. Skilfully she managed the anthropomorphic aspect of her tale: Beatrix's singing, sewing mice are mostly unclothed and Simpkin wears a greatcoat and boots only for his shopping expedition in the snow.

From first draft *The Tailor of Gloucester* resembled a book – a fairy tale written by a soon-to-be-published author. That Beatrix presented her story in this way reflected the newfound confidence of her thirties: growing resolution underlined that confidence. Her altered state of mind had several causes: Warne's interest in Peter Rabbit; the support of Annie Moore and Hardwicke Rawnsley; Beatrix's friendship with Caroline Hutton; her collaboration with Charles McIntosh; even, despite its unsatisfactory outcome, Sir Henry Roscoe's partisanship over her fungus theories. Her thirties were to become for Beatrix a decade of attainment: even her health appeared improved. In her journal on 28 July 1896, Beatrix insisted, 'I feel much stronger at thirty than I did at twenty; firmer and stronger both in mind and body.'[14] Events appeared to corroborate that assessment.

From now on her journal dwelt less minutely on frustrations. There are suggestions that Beatrix had developed means of addressing her parents' fractiousness; and her world expanded physically to accommodate solo visits to family, interviews at Kew Gardens, careful arrangements with London printers over self-publishing. By the time of Freda's letter, with the schoolroom now her studio, Miss Cameron and Mrs A. consigned to memory, designs for Christmas cards and *A Frog he would a-fishing go* issued by commercial publishers and the imminence of Frederick Warne & Co.'s full-colour version of *The Tale of Peter Rabbit*, at last Beatrix could lay claim to an identity of her own inventing and first approaches to independence. Importantly, she had achieved it without compromising outward deference to her parents.

Beatrix Potter fell in love with Norman Warne in the manner of the times: she addressed him first as 'Sir', afterwards as 'Mr Warne'. He became her 'Johnny Crow', named after the active, busy little bird at the heart of Leslie Brooke's illustrated rhyme book, *Johnny Crow's Garden*, which Warne's published in 1903. Beatrix borrowed the nickname from Norman's nieces and nephews. Theirs began as a business correspondence and ended in an engagement. Love was not necessary to the business in hand.

Norman Warne was the youngest of the three surviving sons of Frederick Warne. Three other brothers – Frederick, Alfred and Edwin – had died young. His junior status accounts for his role overseeing *The Tale of Peter Rabbit*, which elder brothers Harold and Fruing labelled slight-ingly Beatrix's 'bunny book'. In 1901 he was thirty-three, two years younger than Beatrix. Like Beatrix he was un-married, the darling of his widowed mother, a doting uncle. Thoughtful and diligent, a keen tennis player and bicyclist, he collected moths. In a basement workshop he essayed small-scale carpentry projects: boxes and cases, eventually a doll's house for his niece Winifred. He was generous-spirited, kind, sometimes self-conscious; in January 1904 he took a family party of ten to the panto-mime – *Humpty Dumpty*, at the Drury Lane Theatre, with Dan Leno as Queen Spritely.

He lived with his mother and unmarried elder sister Millie. The Warnes' large, late-eighteenth-century house in Bedford Square remained a focus for boisterous family parties; unlike the Potters the Warnes relished one an-other's company. Beatrix visited Norman in the offices of Frederick Warne & Co., in Bedford Street, Covent Garden, always in the company of a chaperone. Like Pigling Bland first encountering Pigwig at night in Mr Piperson's kitchen, their behaviour was circumspect – not constrained by fear, as in Pigling's case, but due concern for proprieties. Their courtship – in equal measure Beatrix's doing – was partly epistolary; no one chaperoned their exchange of letters.

A precise quality in Beatrix's character promoted the

relationship. No matter in relation to her books was too small for consideration and so the letters flowed back and forth, cementing regular meetings. Beatrix scrutinised her proofs minutely: she substituted a full stop for a comma; she queried the quality of coloured inks and the hyphenation of words in typesetting; she worried about endpapers, 'something to rest the eye between the cover and the contents of the book; like a plain mount for a framed drawing'.[15] Her early letters are tentative. Beatrix asked questions, requested information, sought guidance, reassurance. Even before publication of *The Tale of Peter Rabbit* on 2 October 1902, she had suggested a second title, a book of rhymes; she busied herself with printing *The Tailor of Gloucester* independently, informing Norman of progress nevertheless. At first, Beatrix's letters to Norman Warne indicate a balance of power tilted in the latter's favour: Norman has the publishing experience, commissions lie in Norman's gift. Her letters go further. Through the written word they construct a dialogue between writer and recipient: they insist on complicity. Beatrix's questions require answers, her suggestions responses, and when her confidence falters, it is clearly Norman's part to reassure her: 'I thought my owls very bad when I went again to the [Zoological] Gardens,' she wrote of preliminary sketches for *The Tale of Squirrel Nutkin*.[16]

Yet Beatrix had inherited her measure of both her grand-fathers' acumen and clear-sightedness. Anthropomorphism on the page did not imply feather-headedness on the author's part. From her earliest letters, Beatrix was attentive to the business aspect of her connection with the Warnes. 'I should wish, before signing an agreement, to understand clearly what arrangement it would imply about the copyright; and what stipulations would be made about subsequent editions, if required,' she wrote in May 1902; her father accompanied her to Bedford Street to inspect contracts.[17] She did not trouble to conceal from Norman the firmness that, in different guises, had always played its part in her make-up: 'I am vexed that the samples of print have not come yet, I hope they will by Monday.'[18] For good and ill, spontaneity undercut formality in Beatrix's letters. Norman Warne can never have been deceived about his newest author's disposition.

It was a measure of Beatrix's growing attachment to Norman that she balanced firmness with concessions, as in the letter she wrote in March 1903 on the subject of an endpaper for *The Tailor of Gloucester* and *The Tale of Squirrel Nutkin*, both of which Warne's planned to publish that Christmas: 'I am afraid I generally say what I think, but I assure you I will draw it any way you like!'[19] Gradually she revealed to Norman the strain of her life at home, her father 'difficult', 'fidgetty' and, in time, 'complaining' (Beatrix blamed 'muscular pain'[20]), her mother so demanding 'it does wear a person out'.[21] It was one approach to intimacy. Within the privacy of a letter she could express what was prevented in person by the repressive chaperonage of Miss Hammond – older now and stone deaf but still vigilant when called upon – or one of her mother's servants.

For the first time since childhood, Beatrix found herself completely occupied. Within fourteen months, Frederick Warne & Co. had issued her stories of Peter Rabbit, Squirrel Nutkin and the Tailor of Gloucester. By the end of 1903, *The Tale of Peter Rabbit* had sold 50,000 copies; Beatrix was a bestselling author, with an income of her own. Her satisfaction had many aspects. Her illustrations had been printed for Warne's by Edmund Evans; in her childhood Evans had printed illustrations by Caldecott, Crane and Greenaway. What Warne's called the 'little books' made Beatrix busier than she could remember. 'Often the mere position of a word makes all the difference in the balance of a sentence,' she explained.[22] She 'took trouble with the words': 'trouble' took time.[23] In addition there were regular visits to Bedford Street and sometimes daily letters to Norman. 'Side-shows' increased her self-imposed workload: Peter Rabbit's Race Game, a board game based on her story; designs for Peter Rabbit wallpaper – Beatrix deliberating between Sanderson and Liberty as her preferred manufacturer; and a Peter Rabbit doll, which she made herself, using the bristles of a broom for whiskers. She registered the doll's patent herself too.

Predictably her parents were not amused by these all-consuming distractions. Rupert's health had begun a steady decline: 'fidgetiness' became curmudgeonly. On 13 July 1903 Beatrix referred to 'such painful unpleasantness at home this winter about the work'.[24] Loyalty did not allow her to elaborate: no elaboration was needed. 'Work' had never featured in the Potters' plans for their only daughter. There are suggestions of pettiness in Rupert and Helen obstructing Beatrix's efforts. Snobbery too. In February 1904, Beatrix declined an invitation from Fruing's wife, Mary Warne. She had been asked for lunch and to look at the doll's house Norman had made for Mary's four-year-old daughter Winifred, to help her with illustrations for *The Tale of Two Bad Mice*. 'I hardly ever go out, and my mother is so "exacting" I had not enough spirit to say anything about it,' Beatrix apologised to Norman.[25] The Fruing Warnes lived in Surbiton, on London's southwest perimeter, a carriage ride from Bolton Gardens. At the age of thirty-eight, Beatrix could not summon either energy or courage to challenge her mother over use of the family carriage. As tactfully as possible, she explained her mother's inevitable distaste for Surbiton.

Any amount of 'unpleasantness' was preferable to returning to that former existence in which she had described herself as 'so much asleep and out of life'. By the summer of 1903, with no new story in hand and the prospect of imminent departure for the Lake District with her parents, Beatrix panicked. 'I had been a little hoping... that something might be said about another book,' she wrote to Norman. 'I could send you a list to consider, there are plenty in a vague state of existence, & one written out in a small copybook.'[26] There is a note of pleading beneath the conversational tone.

For Beatrix, her 'little books' had taken the place of painting and the schoolroom menagerie. With the absorption typical of all her obsessions, she immersed herself wholeheartedly. Candidly she told Norman, 'I do so *hate* finishing books, I would like to go on with them for years.'[27] 'I always feel very much lost when they are finished,' she wrote.[28] Her books offered Beatrix distraction from claustrophobic proximity to her ageing parents, especially what she described, with telling use of inverted commas, as the 'weary business' of the family's 'summer "holiday"'.[29] Those books lay in Norman's gift. In the summer of 1903, at Fawe Park, Keswick, with Norman's agreement, Beatrix began work on sketches for *The Tale of Benjamin Bunny*. In this unlikely fairy story, Norman's encouragement amounted to chivalry of sorts.

On 26 July 1905, Beatrix re-read the end of Jane Austen's *Persuasion*. 'It was always my favourite,' she wrote to Millie Warne afterwards. 'Do you remember Miss Austin's [*sic*] "Persuasion" with all the scenes & streets in Bath?'[30] The previous day Norman Warne had proposed to Beatrix Potter.

Like much in their relationship, it happened by letter. By letter Beatrix accepted Norman. She was days short of her thirty-ninth birthday and had recently finished *The Tale of the Pie and the Patty-Pan*, a comedy of manners that, like *The Sly Old Cat*, addresses the obligations of hospitality and the meaning of generosity. 'With patience and waiting,' she decided, 'my story had come right.'[31] It was not to be.

It had been a cautious courtship, Beatrix shy, reserved and inexperienced emotionally, Norman her match for emotional inexperience with, until then, little visible appetite for female company. At no point had they spent time alone together, even when Beatrix visited Mrs Warne and her unmarried children at home in Bedford Square. Discreetly, their letters reflect their progress towards love.

Two years after their first meeting, Beatrix leavened book business with personal anecdote: 'I had a funny instance of rabbit ferocity last night';[32] acknowledgement of her parents' exactingness provided grounds for sympathy, contrasting with Mrs Warne's treatment of Norman and Millie;[33] Beatrix mentioned the vagaries of her health, including a 'provoking' cold.[34] On 9 November 1903, she described Norman's previous letter as 'kind': her choice of adjective points to the emergence of something more than a working relationship.[35] Six weeks later, she addressed Norman himself as 'Johnny Crow'. She asked him to make her 'a little house' for Hunca Munca. For the briefest instant, her letter tingles with gentle flirtation.[36] By the summer of 1905, Norman had relaxed sufficiently to mention to Beatrix toothache and his visit to the dentist, a more personal revelation a century ago than now.

For her part Beatrix did not conceal from Norman that he had become indispensable to her creative process – 'it sometimes gives me a fresh start to have the drawings looked at'[37] – nor her disappointment when her visits to the offices in Bedford Street were prevented. From Warne's first negotiations for The Tale of Peter Rabbit in 1901, the 'little books' had occupied a central place in Beatrix's life. As Beatrix's editor, Norman had come to share that place. Two decades after the engagements of her cousins Kate,

Blanche and Emily, Beatrix imagined herself Anne Elliot, Norman her Captain Wentworth. After long years of waiting, she had finally achieved emotional fulfilment. 'When any two young people take it into their heads to marry, they are pretty sure by perseverance to carry their point,' Austen asserts. For Beatrix it looked like journey's end.

But her joy proved solitary and short-lived. Hot on the heels of his proposal, Norman fell ill after a sales trip to Manchester. Unaware of the seriousness of his condition, Beatrix attributed it to 'drinking bad water'; she worried nonetheless. On 29 July, the Warnes' doctor ordered bed rest. Norman's absence from the office meant that Beatrix could not arrange to see him for days after accepting his proposal. In the meantime, at home, in terms that did not spare her feelings, Rupert and Helen – especially Helen – made clear their opposition to the match. They had nurtured ambitions for Beatrix's marriage at nineteen: twenty years later, they appear to have consulted their own convenience. Neither, it seemed, wished to give Beatrix up. And that was not all. Helen, living on a cotton-milling fortune, would not condone her daughter's connection with 'trade', whatever the nature of the trade in question; her reaction was extreme. Rupert did not oppose his wife. Beatrix dug in her heels. 'Publishing books is as clean a trade as spinning cotton,' she told Caroline Hutton angrily.[38] Like Mr Tidler in *The Tale of the Faithful Dove*, she 'stuck to [her] post in speechless indignation; [she] threw [her]self into an attitude of defiance'. All in vain: her parents refused to yield. Beatrix agreed not to mention the engagement outside the two families; stubbornly she wore the ring that Norman had given her. A letter to Harold Warne, written on 30 July, suggests something of her perturbation: 'You will not think me very cross if I say I would rather *not* talk much *yet* about that business though I am *very glad* you have been told.'[39] Unnerved by her parents' vehemence, she began to worry that Norman was being precipitate, four years after their friendship had begun.

In the event, Norman's death from lymphatic leukaemia on 25 August prevented further arguments between Beatrix and her parents. Rupert and Helen had opposed their daughter: through no virtue of their own, they had won. At first she had fled from their intransigence to stay with her former governess, Miss Hammond, at the latter's house in West Hampstead. Respite was brief. In the first week of August, as previously arranged, Beatrix accompanied her parents to Llanbedr, a small village on the Welsh coast in Merionethshire, which she described as 'a country of little rough pastures & stone walls'.[40] (That Rupert had left it too late to book his favourite Lake District holiday house, Lingholm, near Keswick, after ten successive holidays in the region may be indicative of his state of mind that fateful summer.) Habit and conditioning were powerful forces in Edwardian family life. Nothing indicates that Beatrix protested against going away with her parents, albeit the diary she resumed in Llanbedr is notable for the amount of time she spent alone. As in the past the Potters travelled by train. An indoor staff of two kitchen maids, two housemaids and a parlour maid accompanied them; the groom, coachman, carriage, a horsebox and two horses made the journey separately.[41] Rupert photographed the family equipage several times during the five-week holiday. Amid narrow lanes and uneven dry-stone walls its appearance is incongruously smart.

Beatrix never saw Norman Warne alive again. A delay in delivering the telegram sent by the Warnes to Llanbedr prevented Beatrix from returning to London in time. In his bedroom at Bedford Square, Norman died on 25 August: for days he had been unable to swallow anything but milk. Beatrix had written to him the day before he died, 'a silly letter all about my rabbits, & the walking stick that I was going to get for him to thrash his wife with.'[42] He was too weak to read it.

She had had her premonitions. Two days earlier she stopped writing her diary. She resumed it after a week, working back through the terrible vanished days that overwhelmed her memory. In this retrospective account, the hills and fields of Merionethshire are full of signs: a stone drinking trough that resembles a coffin, a sick cow, 'lean as two boards with great big eyes', that made her wonder when Norman 'would begin to get hungry and feed up again'.[43] An awful pregnancy shadows her final entry, for the day before Norman died. The landscape is still, as if waiting; all colour has leached out of it, leaving only 'grey light', a 'pearly grey' haze of 'silver sea', a 'leaden colour' over the headland, as if the lifeblood has drained away from the very country itself. 'I remember thinking the evening was as still as death – and as beautiful,' Beatrix writes, before breaking off. 'As I was looking at it there came out through the mist over the sea just for a few seconds – a gleam of golden sunshine – "In the evening there shall be Light" –'.[44]

In adversity she drew succour from the beauty of nature; she looked to the landscape for tatters of reassurance. She retreated behind poetic insipidities, a facile contemporary rhetoric of death, in which suffering and beauty combined and flashes of sunlight offered the balm of divine comfort. Within this careful, conventional idiom Beatrix held powerful emotions in check. She knew now that she had been wrong a decade earlier, when she wrote 'I think men have stronger feelings than women.'[45]

She may not have attended Norman's funeral. A letter

written later suggests she saw his body before burial; afterwards, she visited his grave in Highgate Cemetery, with the new engraving on the family tombstone; she fretted about plants to cheer the plot. Then she left London again for Wales, Gwaenynog in Denbighshire, the home of her uncle-by-marriage, Fred Burton, 'a little old man, deaf, placid, rather dateless, excessively obstinate, very mean as to ha'pence, unapproachably autocratic' and a widower since the recent death of her maternal aunt Harriet Leech.[46] Beatrix travelled with two rabbits, Josey and Mopsy, 'in a small wooden box', and her hedgehog Mrs Tiggy.[47] It was a short visit. She shared Fred Burton's interest in seventeenth- and eighteenth-century furniture, Gwaenynog and its landscape thrilled her, but a house in mourning offered her no comfort.

Early in September she examined second proofs of *The Tale of Mrs Tiggy-Winkle*. She suggested to Harold Warne a new story, *The Tale of Jeremy Fisher*, first outlined in her picture letter to Eric Moore in August 1893 and again, with variations, in a letter to Molly Gaddum, the daughter of her cousin Emily, in October 1895: 'a frog... went fishing and had a bite, but the fish jumped out of the boat before he could put it into his basket.'[48] Work would be her distraction. In the meantime, she snatched time alone; she had her animals for company.

Back in London at the end of the autumn, Beatrix painted the view from the schoolroom window. A monochrome study – light ebbing from the dying day – its dull shadows and the lifeless winter branches of tall trees have a leaden significance. The contrast with a similar view, painted in 1882, showing the distant tower of the Natural History Museum framed by leaves, is marked. She stayed with Mrs Warne and Millie; she painted the Warnes' dining room, the view across Bedford Square, Norman's bedroom. At Christmas she sent Millie a copy of the last sketch she had painted in Llanbedr: a view of a barley field. 'I try to think of the golden sheaves,' she wrote. The image of harvest was painfully at odds with Norman's unnaturally short life and Beatrix would struggle to make sense of her loss; she came to regard Norman as 'a saint'.[49] 'He did not live long,' she wrote to Millie, 'but he fulfilled a useful happy life. I must try to make a fresh beginning next year.'[50]

She kept the engagement ring that Norman had given her, wearing it on her right hand; she kept his pipe and a cache of his letters; she kept his umbrella too for the remainder of her life. 'I think it is a comfort to have pleasant memories, if nothing else,' she told Millie.[51] She did not ask for the return of the engagement present she had given Norman on 1 August, one of the Cinderella illustrations she had completed in 1895. It was a moonlit scene of a pumpkin coach drawn by rabbits. In the Cinderella story, the magic lasts only until midnight, then the accoutrements of fairy tale resume their everyday forms and enchantment vanishes. It was a painful metaphor.

·7·

'A nest right away'

Beatrix in the porch of the restored Hill Top, 1913.

'They came to the river, they came to the bridge –
they crossed it hand in hand – then over the hills
and far away she danced with Pigling Bland!'

The Tale of Pigling Bland, 1913

T HREATENED WITH no escape from the muddle of
his own making – caught in a gooseberry net in Mr
McGregor's garden by the large buttons of his jacket – Peter
Rabbit '[gives] himself up for lost, and shed[s] big tears'. In
the summer of 1905 it was not to be Beatrix's response. She
chose instead to draw succour from what she called 'the
strength that comes from the hills'.[1] She bought a house
and a farm.

Nine years earlier, Rupert Potter had rented a country
house called Lakefield. It was a mid-eighteenth-century
house on a hill, with large windows, a covered veranda
and a walled garden steeply terraced, as well as attics full
of lumber, including 'ancient pistols and an ancient case
and velvet hunting-cap... and a portfolio of chalk drawings, figures and heads, in the style of Fuseli, such as
young ladies drew at school sixty years hence': a treasure

155

trove for Beatrix.[2] Broad views stretched across Esthwaite Water to Langdale Pikes and Grizedale Forest; in good weather and bad, cloud banks dominated the horizon. Beatrix had busied herself with fungi. In an oak coppice, she found 'poor specimens of the poisonous *Agaricus phalloides*'; under a beech tree 'the dark hairy stalks and tiny balls of one of the Mycetozoa'; 'up the steep road towards Grizedale' she sought out inaccessible copses armed with a basket for gathering specimens; she painted the parasol mushroom, *Lepiota procera*.[3] With Bertram she took 'a long dragging walk', relishing the fresh air and the luxuriance of 'wild herbage'. Together the siblings killed a viper with a stick; they cut off its head and noted the tail still twisting and twitching an hour later.[4] Beatrix and her father went out with their cameras; on her own Beatrix drove the carriage about the lanes and through the woods. She emerged unscathed from a collision on a hill that left her 'convulsed with laughter'.[5] In 1900, the Potters returned to Lakefield. On that occasion Beatrix painted a view of the garden, framed by its dramatic landscape setting. Two years later, Beatrix sketched the interior of one of the Lakefield cottages; it became Ribby's cottage in *The Tale of the Pie and the Patty-Pan*. It was at Lakefield that she encountered black Pomeranians too, models for Duchess in the same story.

Subsequently renamed Ees Wyke, Lakefield lies outside

the village of Near Sawrey, which Beatrix first saw in the summer of 1882, during the Potters' tenancy of Wray Castle. In 1896 she renewed her acquaintance with this unspoiled Lancashire hamlet; she noted its 'flowery little gardens' and 'nice old-fashioned people' who lived their lives among the lanes and fields.[6] She concluded that it was 'as nearly perfect a little place as ever I lived in' and never altered her assessment; it joined the lost Edens of Dalguise and Camfield in her imagination.[7] Now, after an interval, she bought a house there – where 'sunshine crept down the slopes into the peaceful green valleys, [and] little white cottages nestled in gardens and orchards'.[8]

Hill Top Farm – an extended seventeenth-century cottage – crouches on a rise of Near Sawrey above the southern stretch of Esthwaite Water, with its distant swathe of mountains and the woods where, afterwards, Beatrix watched charcoal burning. Previously the Potters had lodged their coachman, David Beckett, there, with his wife and children. Beatrix's purchase of Hill Top in the autumn of 1905 represents her final act as a Londoner.

For the house, its 'very overgrown and untidy' garden and thirty-four acres she paid significantly in excess of the market value;[9] she soon learned that, among the villagers, her purchase 'seem[ed] to be regarded as a huge joke'.[10] She was unrepentant. The sale was completed on 25 November, exactly three months after Norman's death. Rupert's solicitors, Braikenridge & Edwards, acted for Beatrix; later she would employ a local firm for property work and conveyancing.[11] Her parents approved the purchase as an investment, as two years earlier they had approved Bertram's acquisition of a farm in Roxburghshire. Glimpsing only a shabby, unadorned North Country farmhouse, with its slate porch, its walls criss-crossed by spindly roses and window-sills crowded with terracotta plant pots like broken teeth, they had no idea that Beatrix meant to live there, along-side Hill Top's resident farm manager, John Cannon and his family – much as they had been unaware that Ashyburn was intended for Bertram's marital home with Mary Scott, the wife he had married in secret on 20 November 1902; Helen never approved of Beatrix living in 'a simple farm house'.[12] A legacy from Helen's sister Harriet Burton supplemented royalties from Beatrix's books to fund the purchase price of £2,805. Although Norman Warne was prevented from seeing its fulfilment, Beatrix's acquisition was surely part of a plan she had discussed with him. A month later, at the more competitive price of £250, she bought an additional field, Buckle Yeat Croft.

In *The Fairy Caravan*, Beatrix describes Tuppenny the guinea pig leaving the town of Marmalade: 'For the first time he smelt the air of the hills. What matter if the wind were chilly; it blew from the mountains.' Lonely in her grief, Beatrix shrugged off London in much the same way. She absorbed herself with self-conscious wholeheartedness in Hill Top and its business: the state of the farm buildings; John Cannon's pig keeping; even the accuracy of the scales used for weighing the Hill Top butter. 'The far end of the orchard is a neglected pretty wilderness, with mossy old trees... and long grass,' she wrote of Codlin Croft Farm in *The Fairy Caravan*. Beatrix doused the Hill Top apple trees with liquid manure, 'a most interesting performance with a long scoop'; she was rewarded when 'the old trees prove[d] to be very good cookers'.[13] 'I have been going over my hill with a tape measure,' she told Harold Warne: every aspect of landownership thrilled her.[14] The success of *The Tale of Mrs Tiggy-Winkle*, lately reprinted, scarcely touched her. She had taken lodgings with the village blacksmith while she formulated her plans. The blacksmith's wife had a new kitten called Tabitha Twitchit.

Beatrix's scheme for Hill Top eventually took the form of a two-storey extension to the house, linked internally by a connecting door. It was her means of providing living quarters for herself – and avoiding 'be[ing] woken up too early by the clank of milk churns'[15] – while retaining John Cannon as farm manager, or 'cowman-foreman-shepherd' in Beatrix's description.[16] (Given Beatrix's inevitable absenteeism while she continued to look after her parents in London, this was an essential measure.) Her extension significantly increased the size of the house and altered its appearance. The legacy of Potter prosperity could not be jettisoned in an instant; in letters written to the Moore children from Sidmouth in 1898 and Winchelsea in 1900, Beatrix had proved her unsuitedness to cottage living. In those instances she described typical country cottages as 'meant for cats and dogs' or resembling 'the little mouse-houses I have often drawn in pictures'.[17] Alongside a new upstairs window, set into the grey pebbledash, Beatrix placed a stone plaque: it is decorated with the date of building work and her initials.

Her plaque was in keeping with vernacular custom; it was also a statement of intent: Beatrix meant to make Hill Top her home. 'For my part I prefer to live in the country,' she wrote in *The Tale of Johnny Town-Mouse* in 1918; the decision was of long standing. Time would increase her conviction that, in the Lake District, she was reconnecting with the 'generations of Lancashire yeomen and weavers; obstinate, hard headed, *matter of fact* folk' from whom, under Jessy Potter's continuing influence, she chose to claim descent.[18]

Beatrix approached her task of improvement and restoration with the minute relish that had characterised her study of insects, fungi and fossils, the same instinct for order she had exhibited as a child cataloguing the habitats and foodstuffs of moth caterpillars. Closely she supervised the layout of new garden paths, the building of garden walls and sturdy oak trellising with acorn finials inspired by fences at Gwaenynog; for the vegetable garden she ordered a wrought-iron gate of art nouveau design. When her instructions for an area of lawn miscarried, Beatrix requested that the tennis-court-size patch be dug up for potatoes; Satterthwaite the village blacksmith fixed up a box hive for bees; she transplanted ferns from a demolished stone bridge into crevices in new garden walls.[19] No matter that she had never gardened before. Gate, vegetable garden and beehive would all shortly feature in Beatrix's 'farmyard tale' of Jemima Puddle-duck; stone walls sprouting ferns play their part in her pictures of Tom Kitten.

To Harold Warne, who had taken Norman's place as her editor, Beatrix outlined a schedule of work on new books. In the spring of 1906 she would complete her story of Jeremy Fisher, before turning her attention to two shorter books for younger children, *The Story of a Fierce Bad Rabbit* and *The Story of Miss Moppet*. Once Beatrix had written to Norman, 'It is pleasant to feel I could earn my own living.'[20] Grief notwithstanding, she remained level-headed. Norman's death had prevented her own story 'com[ing] right... like Anne Elliot's'; she acknowledged an ongoing obligation to her parents, but she did not intend to forfeit the measure of independence represented by her own income, for which she had fought hard. Her letters to Harold were confident and business-like; they illustrate her working practice, as well as her attitude towards her stories. Commending *The Tale of the Faithful Dove* in November 1908, Beatrix explained that it 'ha[d] been lying about a long time, & so have several others'. Unfinished stories exercised a hold on her imagination: 'I should like to get rid of some one of them. When a thing is once printed I dismiss it from my dreams!... But an accumulation of half finished ideas is bothersome.'[21] Long habits of 'thoroughness' balked at incompleteness.

Posterity's version of 'Beatrix Potter' focuses on the eight years Beatrix spent at Hill Top: a sustained burst of intense creativity balanced by her growing knowledge and love of the farmer's life in the North Country. Between 1905 and 1913, she wrote a clutch of her best-known stories: the tales of Tom Kitten, Jemima Puddle-duck, Samuel Whiskers, Ginger and Pickles, the Flopsy Bunnies, Mrs Tittlemouse, Timmy Tiptoes, Mr Tod and Pigling Bland. Hill Top, Near Sawrey and its surrounds provided the setting for most of those stories. Caroline Hutton – married despite earlier protestations and with a small son – remembered accompanying Beatrix 'to find a suitable spot for [Jemima Puddle-duck's] nest'; Beatrix wrote to a little girl in New Zealand that *The Tale of Ginger and Pickles* 'was all drawn in the village near my farm house, and the village shop is there'.[22]

Beatrix herself appears in *The Tale of Samuel Whiskers*, 'going to the post office in the afternoon'; in *The Tale of Pigling Bland*, wearing clogs and a shapeless hat, she pins pig licences 'for safety in [the] waistcoat pockets' of Pigling and his brother Alexander. As previously, she avoided 'imagination in the vulgar sense' by setting her tales in recognisable locales; by 'peopling' her house, garden and farm with her own characters, she blurred the line between fact and fiction. Her inspiration was concrete – like the rat infestation at Hill Top she described to Millie Warne that suggested her story of Samuel Whiskers, or her later need to unburden herself of piglets eating five meals a day, played out in Pigling Bland's story. Her position as omniscient narrator defies the reader to question fictions so studiedly rooted in truth.

At the same time, and threatening to distract her attention from new 'little books', Beatrix's focus on Hill Top resulted in an overhaul of the farm's stock. John Cannon acquired cows, pigs, ducks, chickens and local Herdwick sheep – fourteen pigs, ten cows and thirty-one sheep by Christmas 1908.[23] Partly encouraged by Hardwicke Rawnsley, who in 1899 had founded the Herdwick Sheep Association (the Herdwick Sheep Breeders' Association after 1916), Beatrix would become a leading advocate of this tough local breed, noted for their hardiness and coarse, durable wool. She acquired a small black pig, Sarah, which she treated as a pet: it lived both inside and out, Beatrix 'always afraid [she would] get upstairs one day'.[24] She delighted, too, in her chickens. To Millie Warne, she wrote on 17 November 1909, 'One of the two hens I brought from Sidmouth is the best layer we have ever had, she has had two holidays of ten days; she had laid month after month since February last.'[25] Farm news increasingly dominated Beatrix's letters: a cart house suffering from toothache; an ailing calf treated with chalk mixture, arrowroot and brandy; a sow 'so tame I have to kick her when she wants to nibble my galoshes'.[26] It was a reflection of her shifting priorities.

For much of the year she remained with her parents; she would never occupy Hill Top full time. Her purchases of 'delightful bushes' for the garden – 'lilac, syringa, rhodo-ndendrons [sic], and... a red fuchsia' – and fruit trees to supplement the cooking apples; her plantings in the 'very light drying soil' of phlox, saxifrage, lavender, Japanese anemones and sweet williams given to her by neighbours;[27] and her dealings with plumber, plasterer, joiner and the Cannons all occupied interstices in her life, snatched from the Potters' sedate annual roundelay of seaside and North Country holidays and changeless months in Bolton Gardens. Although she continued to struggle with her parents' exactions, the Beatrix of her forties had ceased to rebel with much vigour. With something closer to equanimity, she wrote, 'It is awkward with old people, especially in winter – it is not very fit to leave them.'[28] For the meantime, escaping to Near Sawrey when she could, she managed to the best of her ability to satisfy conflicting claims. For Christmas 1912, she asked for 'a book about pruning roses'.[29] In her absences, her thoughts were of her garden, an antidote to the 'trying' life she still led with Rupert and Helen. Her love for Hill Top balanced the emotional sterility of home life; it helped bury the agony of bereavement.

For the farm, she built a new barn with 'a large loft above & a stable for calves & bullocks below'.[30] As soon as feasible she moved the Cannons into the new extension. For herself, she began work on the interior of the original cottage: 'a kitchen, a parlour, a pantry and a larder', as in Mrs Tittlemouse's house, and a large square hall from which she removed a later partition wall. Although she did not cook – Beatrix described her culinary skills as restricted to making jam, frying bacon and boiling plain potatoes[31] – she fitted out a new kitchen, with running water laid on; she estimated the costs of her waterworks at fifty pounds. She had walls replastered. As a precaution against rats, zinc panels were fitted to the bottoms of doors and new skirtings made of cement. Against a background of a flower-pattern wallpaper, which even covered the ceiling, she furnished the hall with 'a pretty dresser with plates on it & some old fashioned chairs; & a warming pan that belonged to my grandmother', as well as a set of bellows given to her by Norman. She left in place for now the old-fashioned fireplace range: she had decided to use it in the story she called *The Roly-Poly Pudding* (later renamed *The Tale of Samuel Whiskers*).[32] Throughout the house she hung landscape paintings, adding to her collection over time: a mid-Victorian view of Loch Katrine, the setting for Scott's *The Lady of the Lake*, by Charlotte Nasmyth; a view of Falmouth Harbour, destination for the Potters' spring holiday in 1892, by Pre-Raphaelite painter John Brett; and *Langdale Pikes from Low Wood*, an atmospheric local view painted a century earlier by James Francis Williams. Like her own work, these paintings fictionalised reality: nature transformed and perfected by art.

'If ever I had a house I would have old furniture, oak

in the dining room, and Chippendale in the drawing room,' Beatrix had written in her journal in 1884.[33] At Hill Top she was as good as her word. In the hall she placed an eighteenth-century oak longcase clock and, in 1925, her favourite seventeenth-century oak cupboard, bought expensively at auction: 'very plain, except the middle, fixed panel, which has good carving';[34] she worried she had 'a-fool-of-myself-at-a-sale-made'.[35] She chose mahogany pieces for the panelled parlour and installed an elaborate marble chimneypiece. In 1929, she reimagined the same room as Matilda and Louisa Pussycat's tiny attic parlour in *The Fairy Caravan*, 'containing a polished mahogany table and three chairs with horse-hair seats'; 'silhouette portraits of... ancestors hung on the wall'.[36]

Thanks to the tales of Tom Kitten and Samuel Whiskers, Beatrix's 'cottage' interiors are instantly recognisable. Hers was a vision of its time as much as a rebellion against the ponderous respectability of Bolton Gardens. All her life Beatrix had sketched houses and furniture: the bentwood chair in her bedroom at Camfield Place; an oak dresser at Gwaenynog; the staircase at Lingholm densely hung with pictures; a Gothic table in the library at Wray Castle; back splats and cabriole legs of wooden chairs at Fawe Park, which the Potters rented in 1903. She had a passion for old china, too, showcased in illustrations to *The Tailor of*

Gloucester. At Hill Top, both inside and out, Beatrix gave rein to her enjoyment of the past.

It was an outlook influenced by the Arts and Crafts movement so dear to Hardwicke Rawnsley, a romantic view of pre-industrial England celebrated in illustrations by Caldecott, Greenaway and Crane; Edward Hudson's *Country Life* – begun in 1897 and read by Beatrix intermittently; the watercolours of Helen Allingham and Myles Birket Foster; new attitudes to 'natural' and 'wild' gardening championed by William Robinson and Beatrix's near-contemporary Gertrude Jekyll. In her own words, Beatrix 'appreciate[d] the memories of old times, the simple country pleasures, – the homely beauty of the old farm house, the sublime beauty of the silent lonely hills'.[37] Later she joined the Society for the Preservation of Ancient Buildings, founded by William Morris. She never agreed to the installation of electric lighting at Hill Top or her subsequent home, Castle Cottage.

Beatrix took pains to fit up the house to her liking: she consulted her own taste and her comfort. Above the farmhouse kitchen she built a library for writing and painting; its tall window offered one of Hill Top's best views, up winding Stoney Lane towards Moss Eccles Tarn. Mistress of her own environment for the first time in her life, she may not, like Mrs Tittlemouse, have 'swept, and scrubbed, and dusted' for herself, or 'rubbed up the furniture with beeswax, and polished... little tin spoons'. Like Mrs Tittlemouse, she took pride in possession.

She revelled in Hill Top's irregularities. 'When I lie in bed,' she wrote to Norman's niece Louie Warne, in July 1907, 'I can see a hill of green grass opposite the window about as high as Primrose Hill, and when the sheep walk across there is a crooked pane of glass that makes them look like this [drawings of blurred sheep outlines] and the hens are all wrong too; it is a very funny house.'[38] Her painting of Ribby framed in the hall door with the garden behind her, in *The Tale of Samuel Whiskers*, and of Aunt Petittoes feeding her piglets in the field next to Hill Top, in *The Tale of Pigling Bland*, record the picturesqueness of Beatrix's new Lakeland home. Her parents had furnished their house in London with cumbrous gentility; Beatrix was sincere in her desire to reclaim aspects of her North Country heritage, but her restoration of Hill Top was as much the product of her artist's eye as any of the 'little books'. Sturdy in its landscape, surrounded by its carefully contrived cottage garden, Hill Top became a metaphor for Beatrix's independence: part stage set, part doll's house. She delighted in 'improving' it. She described going 'after dinner to "Tom Kitten's" house [to hang] pictures' in a letter written as late as 1939.[39] The process continued until her death and beyond: in her will she left detailed instructions concerning the furnishing of the house she had never really lived in.

It was the farm that occupied many of her thoughts. In December 1908, from John and Thomas Rigg she bought twenty-two acres of mixed pastureland and woodland close to Far Sawrey. She acquired a further twenty acres the following May, when, for £1,573, she bought Castle Farm. The diminutive farmhouse – scarcely more than a cottage – was visible from the garden of Hill Top. There were outbuildings and another cottage. All were sadly run down. Two years later, in February 1911, she bought an additional small parcel of land adjoining Hill Top, for twenty pounds. A purchase made on 30 December 1913 included a manmade lake or tarn among the sixty-six acres; later Beatrix stocked it with trout and planted water lilies.[40] Her land-buying would continue. In each transaction Beatrix took advice from a local firm of solicitors: W. H. Heelis and Son, of Hawkshead and Ambleside, founded in 1836.

'What a gratifying thing it is in these days to meet with a female devoted to family life!' Beatrix wrote in 1907 in a draft version of *The Tale of Jemima Puddle-Duck.*[41] She herself was among the objects of her irony. Parental expectation had compelled her to devote herself to family life: attentive to filial duty, she acknowledged the ambivalence of that 'devotion' and (at times) the reluctance of her sacrifice. 'I never knew a night go faster,' she had written of an all-night vigil at her mother's bedside in October 1895. In the early hours of the morning, she watched lamplighters and sweeps in the lane outside, 'workmen going to town on bicycles with lights, in the dusk', she was overwhelmed by hunger, but her thoughts did not cling to her mother, despite the latter's serious vomiting and signs of haemorrhage.[42] Ten years later, in the face of parental opposition to her marriage to Norman Warne, she fought doggedly for the chance to devote herself to a family life of her own.

Beatrix in her forties was described as 'quite out of the common... short, blue-eyed, fresh-coloured face, frizzy hair brushed tightly back, dresses in a tweed skirt pinned at the back with a safety pin'.[43] Photographs taken at that time depict a pleasant, rounded face, heavy in repose, with suggestions even in black and white of the 'brilliant colour' that, as a little girl, Millais 'used to provoke on purpose', and an unguarded expression, dullness in her eyes, each socket darkly shadowed.[44] Her hair inclined to unruliness; she dressed as simply as prevailing fashions allowed, mostly without jewellery bar a brooch, in clothes that were practical to the point of shapelessness. Once Millais had described her as 'a little like his daughter, at that time a fine handsome girl'; Rupert had likened her to the portrait of Nina Lehmann, but she had not been brought up to consider herself a beauty and she paid little attention to her appearance. With age she had grown heavier. To an American visitor, who took her photograph in May 1913, Beatrix wrote in some surprise, 'I am wondering if I really am quite so fat as the stout female with my very small ducklings appears to be.'[45] She did not change her ways. In time, her lack of interest in dress would appear an eccentricity. In the eyes of North Country gentry, Beatrix's simple tweeds and the wooden-soled leather clogs she seldom removed were better suited to village slatterns than a woman of property and independent fortune.

The man who became Beatrix Potter's husband in October 1913 was not concerned by her dress. He was a quiet man like Norman Warne and, like Norman, disinclined to dominate. 'There was an ambience about him,' noted one observer, 'of an eighteenth-century quiet gentleman.'[46] Beatrix described him as 'dreadfully shy'. Tall, slightly stooping, he had a kindly face. 'When I want to put William in a book – it will have to be as some very tall thin animal,' she wrote.[47]

William Heelis was the youngest of eleven children of the late Reverend John Heelis of Kirkby Thore near

Appleby and his wife Esther Martin; his grandfather and great-grandfather had also been Anglican priests. Since 1900, he had been a partner in the Hawkshead office of W. H. Heelis and Son. He worked alongside his cousin, William Dickinson Heelis; to avoid confusion, William Heelis was known as 'Appleby Billy', William Dickinson Heelis as 'Hawkshead Willie'. Their relationship may not have been straightforward: the men exchanged few visits outside office hours. 'Appleby Billy' was a keen sportsman: he played bowls and golf, the latter, Beatrix reported afterwards, sometimes late into Saturday evenings; he enjoyed folk dancing and rode a motorcycle. When opportunity allowed he shot; a gun dog for William would be added to the tally of Beatrix's animals. The *Westmorland Gazette* described him as 'one of the best all-round sportsmen in the Lake District'.

William Heelis proposed to Beatrix four years after she became his client, a period in which they had spent more time apart than together. Together they had discussed Beatrix's farm plans; William had explained the esoterica of land law. In driving rain, in snow, in summer sun, they had walked Beatrix's pastures and new fields. Companionship came before love: shared interests bred familiarity. As Beatrix had associated Norman with her 'little books', William was associated with Near Sawrey: she did not require his participation in her 'other' life as 'Beatrix Potter'. As a cousin noted later, 'they shared each other's interest in sheep and farming and the love of the beautiful Lake District'.[48] And there are signs that Beatrix had not abandoned thoughts of marriage entirely, despite the lingering sorrow of Norman's loss. In the winter of 1909, a boy called Andrew Fayle wrote to her about a wife for Jeremy Fisher. Beatrix replied with a series of witty miniature letters. 'I live alone; I am not married. When I bought my sprigged waistcoat & my maroon tail-coat, I had hopes... But I am alone.' She signed her letter 'Jeremiah Fisher'. With characteristic wryness, she added, 'If there were a "Mrs Jeremy Fisher" she might object to snails. It is some satisfaction to be able to have as much water & mud in the house as a person likes.'[49] In a subsequent letter, written from 'Alderman Ptolemy Tortoise', Beatrix suggests, 'I am of opinion that [Jeremy Fisher's] dinner parties would be much more agreeable if there were a lady to preside at the table.'[50]

Through the rain-sodden family holiday of 1912, in a rented house on Windermere that kept her too often from Hill Top, the idea of William's proposal sustained Beatrix; she was frustrated at her enforced absence from the farm. 'It is such hard work toiling backwards and forwards to Sawrey, especially in this terrible weather – that I seem to have little time or energy to go anywhere else,' she wrote;

to Millie, she confessed 'the going backwards and forwards takes it out of me'.[51] From a distance she bickered with Harold Warne over the text of *The Tale of Mr Tod*, particularly her opening paragraph with its reference to 'disagreeable people'; afterwards she was irritated by the book's endpapers: 'perfectly horrible – too big, and rather commonplace'.[52] Neither the story's undoubted quality nor the success of its predecessors offered any solace. It was a difficult summer, characterised for Beatrix by an all-enveloping sense of fatigue; she made no new sketches. Inevitably, there was worse to come.

The Potters had disapproved of Norman Warne; they disapproved of William Heelis. Again, self-interest sharpened snobbery: without Beatrix in constant attendance they could no longer manage Bolton Gardens. This time the Heelises returned their disapprobation. Beatrix's Unitarianism was a stumbling block; so, too, her disdain for social convention and her dislike of everyday social life. 'I eschew tea parties,' she told her cousin Caroline; witheringly she described the social life of Hawkshead as 'nothing but gossip and cards'.[53] Eventually a silver cream jug was proffered as a wedding present. Beatrix's response lacked emollience: 'If you give me a cream jug, I'll throw it out of the window, I can't abide them!'[54] It was not an attitude to inspire affection.

Back at Bolton Gardens, Christmas was more than usually sombre. Rupert had a severe cold. 'When old people are ill they do grumble, even more than necessary,' Beatrix reported feelingly.[55] Weeks later it was her own turn to fall ill. Her sickness became acute. By the first week of March, she could hardly hold a pen and her letters to Harold Warne were written for her. 'I have been resting on my back for a week as my heart has been rather disturbed by the Influenza,' she explained to him. She was incapable of work on the latest 'little book', which would become *The Tale of Pigling Bland*. Six weeks later her recovery remained only partial: 'I seem to take such a long time to get strong again.'[56] Welcome distraction came in the form of proofs of Victorine Ballon's French translation of *The Tale of Peter Rabbit*, which Beatrix approved. At Hill Top at the end of April she was stopped in her tracks by breathlessness while trying to walk up 'a short hill'.

But Beatrix's mind was made up. With an effort she finished *Pigling Bland* and dispatched her manuscript to Harold Warne. She insisted later that there was nothing autobiographical in Pigling and Pigwig escaping their pursuers 'over the hills and far away'. Lacking vanity and feminine wiles, it is impossible that Beatrix should choose to depict herself in the guise of 'a perfectly lovely little black Berkshire pig', one of the most incorrigible coquettes in children's literature, or stoop to the coyness of likening herself to 'a little round ball, fast asleep on the hearth-rug'. But her insistence on a happy ending for her story – and the pigs' escape from conventional expectation – surely reflects her resolution and something of the optimism this resolution inspired in her. After a rush to finish the illustrations, the book was published days ahead of Beatrix's wedding.

Beatrix Potter and William Heelis were married on 15 October 1913 at the church of St Mary Abbots, Kensington Church Street. The only guests bar Rupert and Helen were Beatrix's friend Gertrude Woodward, daughter of the Keeper of Geology at the British Museum, and Willie's best man, a cousin based in Oxford; the *Westmorland Gazette* described the ceremony as conducted in 'the quietest of quiet manners'. Bertram remained in Scotland. In May he had come to Beatrix's aid in dramatic fashion, countering his parents' protests against Willie's unsuitability with the revelation of his own secret marriage, now of eleven years' duration, to Mary Scott. Even though he stalled at disclosing full details of Mary's background as a wine merchant's daughter and former textile mill worker, Bertram's intervention went some way to unravelling the family impasse.

The previous day Beatrix and William had sat for photographs by Rupert in the garden at 2 Bolton Gardens. Both wore country tweeds, William with bulging pockets, Beatrix every bit as stout as she had feared back in May. Neither possessed in any measure Jeremy Fisher's sartorial élan, his 'sprigged waistcoat &... maroon tail-coat'. Beatrix was pictured with – and without – an elaborate flowered hat. She was forty-seven years old; William was forty-two. Her expression is one of contentment rather than euphoria. Her fondness for William, she wrote, had increased with parental opposition: his feelings likewise. To Millie Warne, in a letter that cannot have been easy to write, she had explained in July that it was 'the miserable feeling of loneliness that decided me at last'.[57] She did not mention love; her chances of motherhood were past. If Beatrix's marriage contained an element of compromise, she did not betray it. Her letters do not suggest misgivings.

To a little girl who shortly wrote to offer her congratulations, Beatrix replied enclosing a piece of wedding cake and a copy of her newest book. She was at pains to point out that 'the portrait of two pigs arm in arm – looking at the sun-rise – is not a portrait of me & Mr Heelis'. It was, she conceded, 'a view of where we used to walk on Sunday afternoons!'[58] On 25 October, *Country Life* published 'The Fairy Clogs', one of four unillustrated short stories Beatrix had written in 1911; it appeared under the banner headline 'Tales of Country Life'. The name 'Beatrix Potter' did not appear. Instead the author was identified using Beatrix's new initials: H. B. H. In public as well as in private she had embarked on her life as Mrs Heelis.

· 8 ·

'A large interesting farm'

On 14 October 1913, the day before her wedding, Rupert Potter photographed Beatrix and Willie Heelis in the garden at Bolton Gardens.

'When the sun comes out again, you should see
my garden and the flowers... no noise except the
birds and bees, and the lambs in the meadows'

The Tale of Johnny Town-Mouse, 1918

'AFTER I MARRIED I just locked the door and left,' Beatrix
claimed of Hill Top in 1913 – like Pigling Bland and
Pigwig stealing quietly away from Mr Piperson's kitchen.[1]
She chose not to live with William at Hill Top, cheek by
jowl with the Cannons, in the rooms she had fitted up to
suit herself. Instead, in the second half of 1913, she set in
train building work and extensive renovations at Castle
Cottage: 'new rooms... the staircase is altered, & we are
going to have a bathroom'.[2]

As at Hill Top Beatrix's wholesale alterations transformed the small Lakeland homestead. The house more
than doubled in size. Beatrix moved the front door; she
built a large first-floor room with views across the sloping
garden. Mrs Cannon became 'dairywoman farm housekeeper', with responsibility for the rooms Beatrix left
behind her. Hill Top is clearly visible from Castle Cottage

and Beatrix walked easily between the two; in the library at Hill Top, called the New Room, she still wrote and painted at the old bureau bookcase. Beatrix's image of locking the door and leaving is misleading. In October 1913, she did not exchange one way of life for another, nor did a chapter of her life abruptly close: she was accustomed to multiple existences. In her first years as Mrs Heelis of Castle Cottage, as at Hill Top as Miss Potter, Beatrix continued to balance the various claims of family life, the 'little books' and her farm.

In 1891, at Putney Park, she had come face to face with Jemima Blackburn, author of *Birds Drawn from Nature*. Beatrix had judged her 'a broad, intelligent observer with a keen eye for the beautiful in nature, particularly in plant-world life, as well as for the humorous.'[3] The description applies as securely to Beatrix herself. Her 'keen eye for the beautiful in nature' had shaped her restoration of Hill Top and the garden she made there; sharpened by humour, it inspired all the 'little books'. She did not embark on marriage intent on closing behind her the door onto her work as a children's author, any more than she meant to settle for the tea-and-cards routine of the country solicitor's wife or absorb herself exclusively in farm concerns.

She had bought Hill Top at a moment of overwhelming sadness. 'Planting cuttings of rock plants on the top of the garden wall', driving the trap to Hawkshead to watch 'the black sea-ducks swimming & diving' on a lake 'as smooth as glass', lighting for the first time the new library fire and imagining children's games of hide-and-seek in 'funny cupboards & closets' had soothed her in the empty aftermath of Norman's death.[4] For the first time, she had laid out and planted a garden of her own; she had watched the milking of the cows, with their foolish names – Kitchen, White Stockings, Garnett, Rose, Norah and Blossom; despite her ineligibility as a woman to vote, she had interested herself for the first time in local elections, at Kendal and Windermere. Hill Top had moulded Beatrix's writing and her painting. It had allowed her to develop fully a personal vision, untrammelled by outside pressures, and it became for Beatrix a reflection and an extension of herself: 'the deepest me, the part one has to be alone with'.[5] In all weathers she painted the Hill Top views – the hills and fields and trees; she painted harvest times of corn stooks, and the roofs and chimneystacks that surrounded her, continually adding to the kaleidoscopic portfolios of 'very scribblesome' background sketches she had assembled since Miss Hammond's sway in the schoolroom; she squirrelled them out of sight behind the geyser in the bathroom.[6] A clutch of 'little books' celebrated the completeness of Beatrix's engagement with house, farm and village community.

This imaginative absorption, which never dwindled, was itself akin to a marriage: every bit as binding as Beatrix's union with William Heelis.

In turn the 'little books' had enabled Beatrix to improve and extend her landholdings. Her life had grown like the plants in her garden, nurtured by so 'perfect a little place' and 'lovely spring[s] of blossoms, [when] the hawthorn bushes were like snow, and the bluebells like a bit of sky come down'.[7] Piecemeal, like a patchwork quilt, she had added to her farm. In spite of her role at her parents' side, her skills as author-illustrator had matured through the 'Sawrey' and 'Hill Top' books, guaranteeing substantial royalty payments from Warne's. Her neighbours recognised and appreciated Beatrix's renown; her letters indicate their competitiveness to be included in her stories. At the time of her marriage to William Heelis, Beatrix could look proudly on the life she had made for herself in the Lake District. She had even partly emerged from domestic attrition with her parents. That the remainder of her life was chiefly occupied in farming and conservation was not an inevitable consequence of her marriage in 1913. Beatrix's self-identity – which once her parents had persuaded her was self-will – was strong enough to embrace varied personae simultaneously. She was proud of her married status and insisted on being addressed as 'Mrs Heelis'. That she maintained

Hill Top as a private preserve, an expression of 'the deepest me' – in the words of one visitor in 1927 'a little museum unchanged forever from the time of the books' – and described it in letters to children and admirers of her books as 'Tom Kitten's house', is proof of a different sort of pride: in the achievements of 'Beatrix Potter'.[8]

She began her married life with experiments in cooking, guided by Mrs Beeton, Millie Warne's wedding present; William helped her. She darned his socks and spent her first married Christmas with a gaggle of Heelises at Battlebarrow House, Appleby; she forged particular friendships with William's nieces. And she planned a new story, rich in mischief and humour.

It revisited the theme of pursuer and pursued, which Beatrix had first treated in *The Tale of Peter Rabbit*. She borrowed elements of fairy tale, notably the story of Puss-in-Boots; again she satirised self-importance and snobbery. Among her illustrations would be scenes of rough shooting: she asked Willie to pose, gun in hand, to prevent problems that had marred illustrations in *The Tale of the Fierce Bad Rabbit*. To Harold Warne, whose response was unexpectedly muted, Beatrix explained, 'It is about a well-behaved prim black Kitty cat, who leads rather a double life, and goes out hunting with a little gun on moonlight nights, dressed up like puss in boots.' She added that, 'as the gun is only a pop gun (which continually goes off), the bag is neither large nor painful'.[9]

In March 1914, despite laggardly builders and the '*awful mess*' at Castle Cottage, and with a semblance of her old enjoyment, Beatrix made a start on her drawings. Four months later, however, she had made no progress. 'I am interested in the drawings again – in the sense of getting my mind on it, and feeling I could make something of it – if only I had time & opportunity,' she lamented.[10] Ever since the purchase of Hill Top, time and opportunity had conspired to thwart her. Now, for the first time, Beatrix's difficulties proved insurmountable.

She was a wealthy woman, preeminent in her field, her reputation assured, the most successful author Warne's published, in her own words 'well off independently! so long as the books continue to sell'.[11] Even Rupert had described himself in 1910 as 'proud of my daughter's freshness of humour which has never yet become dull' – albeit not to Beatrix herself.[12] Yet she remained wife and daughter as well as author. When Rupert's health declined sharply at the end of 1913, it was Beatrix's clear duty to support both her parents.

Rupert Potter was suffering from stomach cancer. He died, at the age of eighty-two, on 8 May 1914. For five months Beatrix had moved between Castle Cottage and

Bolton Gardens. Although the Potters employed professional nurses, limiting the amount of time Beatrix was
confined to her father's bedside, she was understandably
relieved when 'he went suddenly at the end'.[13] She had not
left him for the final week. She inherited £35,000, the bulk
of the executor's task of overseeing her father's estate, and
the problem of what to do with her mother. She also inherited Rupert's cameras and photographic equipment, surely
a belated testamentary compliment.

It was impossible to leave Helen on her own. Beatrix
arranged a companion in the form of an elderly aunt. She
rented houses in Sawrey for both women, evidently to
William's alarm, as well as for Helen's coachman. A year
later, Lindeth Howe, a solid, gabled Victorian villa on a
hill above Windermere, with glasshouses including a cool
greenhouse for cacti, came onto the market. The Potters
had rented the house in the summer of 1911 and again in
1913; with Beatrix's encouragement, Helen bought it. A care-
taker was installed in Bolton Gardens, Harrods employed
for removals, and the Potters' London servants – in addition
to Beckett the coachman, four maids and a 'tween maid –
resettled by Beatrix at Lindeth Howe; she went on to hire
two gardeners. 'It took me two months to move Mother's
possessions from No. 2 Bolton Gardens,' she wrote.[14] Gently,
in words mostly unspoken, Beatrix negotiated the terms of

her continuing responsibility to her seventy-six-year-old mother – initially, near-constant errands that kept her 'on the trot', afterwards a pattern of regular, more-than-weekly visits. Helen adapted to her new existence of needlework and pet canaries; ruefully Beatrix pointed to her 'good lungs, no rheumatism and good eyesight'.[15] With William busy in the office in Hawkshead, and a farm to oversee, it was not surprising that Beatrix made no headway with the story she had provisionally entitled *The Tale of Kitty-in-Boots*. 'I do wish I had got more done last winter before interruptions began,' she lamented to Harold Warne. Unusually, this stubborn and self-contained woman asked for sympathy: 'It is very difficult to keep up to a fixed level of success.'[16]

Since publication of *The Tale of Peter Rabbit* in 1902, Beatrix had completed nineteen 'little books', often at a rate of two a year. She had steeped herself in writing after Norman's death as part of the 'fresh beginning' she had promised herself – just as long ago she had banished sleeplessness by committing to memory whole plays by Shakespeare. That unrelenting schedule represented an act of will: on 11 August 1908, she wrote, 'I have been trying dreadfully hard to think about another story about "Peter". I thinked and thinked and thinked last year; but I didn't think enough to fill a book!'[17] Her 'little books' had offered an emotional outlet in an arid private life:

they counterbalanced her parents' 'fidgetting' and queru-
lousness. Now, at another moment of personal strain, her
confidence in her ability to maintain freshness and inspiration faltered. In 'The Fairy Clogs' and in other unpublished
writing for an older audience – stories called 'Carrier's Bob',
'Pace Eggers' and 'The Mole Catcher's Burying' – she had
made first attempts at writing fiction without illustrations.
In 1914 the urgency of her involvement with her writing
was correspondingly less. Beatrix had William; she had
Hill Top and Castle Cottage; she had her farms, 'the ideal
beauty' of the Lake District.[18] The 'silent air on the hills'
sustained her.[19]

In a letter written in March 1916, Beatrix described herself
as 'very active and cheerful'.[20] By then, her farm accounted
for much of her activity; aside from her marriage, it was
also her principal source of cheer. With ironic asperity she
had written to *The Times* following the founding earlier
that year of the Women's National Land Service to provide
female farm labour during the First World War. She signed
her letter 'A Woman Farmer'. 'I have worked on [my farm]
for years and love it,' she wrote. To her old friend Hardwicke
Rawnsley, she described herself simply as 'a farmer'.

At first Beatrix's personal disappointment at her inability

to complete more than a single illustration for *The Tale of Kitty-in-Boots* bit hard. She blamed failing eyesight, which was troubling her more and more – 'my eyes are gone so long sighted & not clear nearby';[21] uncharacteristically she blamed Harold and Fruing Warne and their lack of interest in the story. Once war broke out, in August 1914, she blamed short-handedness on the farm, which forced her to take on more physical work herself. Increasing short-sightedness was undoubtedly a factor: from this point on her sketches and paintings lack the precision and sharp focus of her earlier work and the quality declines. She used the war as an excuse for not visiting a London optician. And in August 1916, having abandoned Kitty-in-Boots, she admitted that her plan to revive a story she had first illustrated in rough as a present for Harold's youngest daughter Nellie in March 1906 was beyond her. She requested that her sketches for *The Sly Old Cat* be worked up by another illustrator, and suggested Ernest Aris, who had recently published *Mrs Beak-Duck*, modelled closely on Jemima Puddle-duck; his recommendations in Beatrix's eyes were 'considerable technical facility and no originality'.[22] The subtext of Beatrix's letters is clear: she had come to view the 'little books' as a chore. 'I painted most of the little pictures to please myself. The more spontaneous the pleasure – the more happy the result,' she wrote in 1940.[23] But the experience of *The Tale of Kitty-in-Boots* had denied spontaneous pleasure; the results were unhappy.

Beatrix's disaffection was more than frustration at 'eyes that... are beginning to feel anno domini'.[24] For several years her dealings with Frederick Warne & Co. had become less satisfactory. Harold was dilatory about royalty statements and erratic in making Beatrix's payments; he failed to capitalise on potentially lucrative merchandising opportunities, the 'side shows' that Beatrix had always treated seriously, including, in the spring of 1914, suggestions for notepaper and almanacs featuring Potter characters. Beatrix's own accounts were disordered: 'I am completely at large about the position, & I filled in income tax at random'.[25] Given her customary astuteness and a financial sharpness to match that of Tabitha Twitchit's shopkeeping in *The Tale of Ginger and Pickles*, it was not a position she relished. By the middle of 1915, she was four years behind in her records. In an emphatic letter to Fruing, she labelled the muddle 'a trial of patience'.[26] Later she claimed that Harold had been 'a trial' to her 'for many years' and refused to allow him any opportunity for 'meddling' in dealings connected with the 'little books'.[27]

Correctly she suspected malpractice on Harold's part. She had no idea that what she imagined a lack of organisation amounted to forgery on a criminal scale. Despite possessing what *The Times* described as 'the highest reputation', Harold was arrested in London on 2 April 1917. Three weeks later, the paper reported, he was sentenced 'to 18 months' imprisonment with hard labour on a charge, to which he pleaded "Guilty", of forging and uttering an acceptance to a bill of exchange for £985 14s. and the acceptance to another bill.'[28] Harold's lawyer stressed that Fruing had known nothing of Harold's attempts to divert money from Frederick Warne & Co. to William Fruing & Co., an ailing fishing business based on Jersey, which the elder brother had inherited on his mother's death in 1908.

Fruing's ignorance notwithstanding, Harold's forgeries, totalling £20,000, had brought the publishing house to the brink of bankruptcy. To prevent foreclosure Fruing sold his house and the bulk of his possessions; he sold his watch and his signet ring; to neighbours he sold the doll's house that Norman had made for his daughter Winifred, the setting for Beatrix's story of Tom Thumb and Hunca Munca. He set about restructuring the company and promptly dispatched to Beatrix the errant royalty statements that had originally spiked her concern. Six months later, he published Beatrix's first 'little book' for four years: *Appley Dapply's Nursery Rhymes*. A revised version of *Peter Rabbit's Painting Book*, first devised by Beatrix in 1911, appeared the same month. By late November, following a second imprint, Warne's had issued 35,000 copies of *Appley Dapply*. Truthfully Beatrix told him, 'I am *very glad* to hear the new book has caught on.'[29]

It was not her best book, not even the book she had intended when, a lifetime ago, at the time of *The Tale of Peter Rabbit*, she had suggested to Norman a rhyme book. Quoting the proverb 'half a loaf is better than no bread' by way of apologia, Beatrix had ransacked her portfolios to offer Fruing a mixed assortment of illustrations, some of them dating as far back as 1891. 'The old drawings are some of them better than any I could do now,' she explained. To another correspondent, she wrote, 'The pictures were done a long time ago – I have little time for painting now, & I have to wear spectacles.'[30] She worried there was a 'shabby' quality to the enterprise, which was prompted mostly by attachment to Norman's family firm. Certainly there is something familiar about *Appley Dapply's Nursery Rhymes*, like a roundup of Beatrix's schoolroom favourites: pictures of mice, rabbits, a guinea pig and a hedgehog. Presciently the narrator of the rhyme of Cottontail and the black rabbit asks, 'She's heard it before?' The book's frontispiece was one of the designs for Christmas cards Beatrix had sold to Hildesheimer & Faulkner in 1894.

Beatrix attributed *Appley Dapply's* success to people wanting 'a cheerful present for children' as the war dragged on and, on 17 October 1917, offered Fruing 'another book of rhymes for next year'.[31] When Fruing demurred, she came up with an alternative, a 'mouse story' inspired by Aesop, reimagined in Hawkshead. It became *The Tale of Johnny Town-Mouse*, published in 1918, the best of her later stories. The extent of Warne's exigency is revealed by the speed of publication. The book was produced in time for Christmas, despite Beatrix only delivering final illustrations in late August.

As with *Appley Dapply's Nursery Rhymes*, the success of *The Tale of Johnny Town-Mouse* spurred Beatrix on. In February 1919, she told Fruing Warne, 'I have been thinking out a new book... I will send you a rough plan soon.'[32] It was a second Aesop-inspired story, *The Tale of Jenny Crow*. Fruing baulked. He suggested returning to *The Tale of the Faithful Dove*. Beatrix took offence. She changed the story's title to *The Tale of the Birds & Mr Tod*, but Fruing remained unenthusiastic. Too late he understood his mistake: in May 1920 Beatrix gave up the idea entirely. Ambitiously she suggested a collaboration with Archibald Thorburn, the Scottish watercolourist who annually designed Christmas cards for the Royal Society for the Protection of Birds: nothing else could tempt her back to *The Faithful Dove*.[33] Her final offer was a reiteration of her earlier suggestion of 'a companion volume to Appley [*sic*] Dapply'. In November

1919, correspondence between author and publisher included an ominous threat on Beatrix's part: 'you don't
suppose I shall be able to continue these d...d little books
when I am dead and buried!! I am utterly tired of doing
them, and my eyes are wearing out. I will try to do one
or two more for the good of the old firm; but it is quite
time I had a rest from them.'[34] To a niece of William's she
wrote, 'I can assure you of one thing, I should be only too
delighted to see a successor.'[35]

Beatrix kept her promise to Fruing. In 1922, the restruc-
tured Frederick Warne & Company Limited published
Cecily Parsley's Nursery Rhymes; in 1930, after a lengthy interval, *The Tale of Little Pig Robinson*, conceived in Ilfracombe
in 1883, became Beatrix's twenty-third and last 'little book'.
Poor eyesight and the excessive workload of the upland fell
farmer prompted Beatrix's virtual withdrawal from publishing. Dwindling confidence in her abilities also played
its part, mishandled by publishers who failed to recognise
that, despite occasional brusqueness, as well as international acclaim, Beatrix still required reassurance.

'It is much easier for me to attend to real live pigs &
rabbits; after all I have done about 30 books, so I have
earned a holiday,' Beatrix wrote to an overseas acquaintance
in November 1920.[36] It was partly a face-saving statement
and, despite the satisfaction of her farming life, included

its measure of wistfulness. As she wrote later, her philosophy was 'to make the best of the present'; she dismissed slights and disappointments as 'raindrops on the sand'.[37]

Aged seventeen, Beatrix had referred in her journal to 'those grumblers the farmers'.[38] Thirty years later and a farmer herself, she too was inclined to grumble – provoked by labour shortages, increased red tape and wide-ranging deprivations brought about by the Great War. 'I have a big farm and a very great deal to do, since the war, for my men left me, and now I have an old shepherd, 2 boy & 2 girls, which requires more looking after,' she wrote in December 1917. She inventoried her livestock as a sheepdog called Fleet, Dolly the pony, '3 horses... 14 cows, a lot of calves & young cattle, and 80 ewes & 40 young sheep & some pigs & 25 hens & 5 ducks, & there *were* 13 turkeys.'[39] To a niece of William's she offered the blander, but to Beatrix truthful, description of 'a large interesting farm'.[40] Of its 120 acres at the start of the war, less than a tenth was given over to arable; the rest consisted of hill pastures and meadow hay.

Beatrix became farm owner first, farmer second. Until his retirement in 1919, John Cannon managed the farm at Hill Top; his sons' wartime call-up prompted Beatrix's greater involvement with day-to-day tasks. She 'look[ed]

after the poultry & rabbits and pony and [her] own particular pet pig'; time permitting, she weeded the turnips.[41]
She acquired her knowledge of farming piecemeal, partly
through her correspondence with Bertram, to whom she
remained deeply attached despite their physical separation.
As in her earlier wide-ranging study of natural history, she
was largely self-taught. 'I flatter myself that I have learnt to
make hay,' she told a sister-in-law in August 1916, much as
she had taught herself fungus identification or the distinctive way in which, in different species of trees, 'the branches
grow from a trunk'.[42] She was also similarly thorough. Faced
by fluke infestation in her flocks in the 1920s, she took to
examining sheep dung under the microscope for parasites.

Beatrix explained once to a prospective farm worker,
'I don't depend on the farm for a living.'[43] Throughout her
farming life, royalties from her 'little books' and from 'side
shows' as varied as Peter Rabbit slippers and handkerchiefs,
subsidised farm incomes, a makeweight against the unpre-
dictability of poor harvests and fluctuating cattle and wool
prices. The extent of those royalties afforded her considerable scope. In the last two decades of her life, '"written
out" for story books', her eyes 'tired for painting',[44] Beatrix
exploited that scope to celebrate her love of landscape
in a manner every bit as enduring as the vision of the
'little books'.

· 9 ·

'The company of gentle sheep, and
wild flowers and singing waters'

Beatrix with shepherd Tom Storey, farm manager at Hill Top, and a prize-winning Herdwick ewe at an agricultural show in the Lake District, c. 1930.

'This looks like the end of the story, but it isn't'

The Tale of Squirrel Nutkin, 1903

TIME WOULD PROVE to Beatrix that she had been mistaken, aged fifteen, in her conviction that 'man may spoil a great deal, but he cannot change the everlasting hills, or the mighty river, whose golden waters still flow on at the same measured pace, mysterious, irresistible'.[1]

She had witnessed man's 'spoiling' at Dalguise in 1884, 'things more dilapidated than ever... deaths and changes, and the curse of drink... heavy on the land'; she had seen for herself the impermanence of nature, 'some saplings grown, others dead. Here and there a familiar branch fallen.'[2] Hardwicke Rawnsley, intimately concerned with landscape preservation since the early 1880s, had repeatedly drawn her attention to the impact on the country of irresponsibility and greed. She had made donations to Rawnsley's appeals on behalf of the National Trust, including, in 1913, the purchase of Queen Adelaide's Hill, where

William IV's widow had landed on her visit to Windermere in 1840, with unspoiled views over the north end of the lake. Rawnsley had impressed upon Beatrix the need to safeguard communities and ways of life, in some instances by intervention. He influenced her later wish 'to preserve some portions of wild land unspoilt for the general good': 'the little larch-wood, deliciously cool, and a gentle sound of the stream below',[3] the banks 'full of wild flowers; wood sorrel, spotted orchis, dog violets, germander, speedwell, and little blue milkwort', 'the little white farm houses and green fields in the dales'.[4] At Camfield, at Dalguise and in the Lake District, 'land unspoilt' provided the backdrop to Beatrix's happiest memories.[5] For Beatrix, there was an emotional dimension to landscape.

She played her own part, independent of Rawnsley's promptings. In 1912, she campaigned vigorously – and successfully – against 'a beastly fly-swimming spluttering aeroplane careering up & down over Windermere' and the threat of an aeroplane factory on wooded lakeshore at Cockshutt Point. In a picturesque letter published in *Country Life* on 13 January, she described its propeller as resembling 'millions of blue-bottles, plus a steam threshing machine'; she wrote letters to *The Times*. She organised twin petitions, exploiting her multiple identities: under the signature 'H. B. Potter' she canvased support nationally, including London publishers; she signed a version for local circulation 'H. B. Potter, *farmer*'.[6] Fifteen years later, Cockshutt Point was again under threat – at 'immenent [*sic*] risk of disfigurement by extensive building and town extension'.[7] The National Trust launched an appeal. In its support, Beatrix did what Fruing Warne could no longer persuade her to and painted fifty rabbit pictures, copied from illustrations to *The Tale of Peter Rabbit*. She sent them to the Bookshop for Boys and Girls in Boston, Massachusetts. Each raised a guinea towards the appeal.

She was not an instinctive polemicist. She had achieved success as the creator of children's books that avoided the overt didacticism of much of her own childhood reading. In a small way she had protested in the past at what she regarded as foolish or iniquitous. Ahead of the 1910 general election, irritated by Peter Rabbit dolls imported from Germany at prices that undercut British manufacturers, she drew and circulated nearly sixty posters in favour of tariff reform, opposing free trade; she described her fingers as 'rather stiff' and 'tired of drawing'.[8] One poster shows a doll in front of a tombstone – 'Here lies the South London Toy Trade killed by Free Trade with Germany'. The same year, she paid for 2,000 copies of a leaflet protesting at a proposed government horse census. Beatrix suspected horse conscription in the event of war; she feared the damaging impact on farming of the forcible removal of horse stock.

She signed 'The Shortage of Horses' leaflet 'North Country Farmer'. Averse to advertisement for her books or publicity for herself, and adept at compartmentalisation, she resisted capitalising on her reputation as 'Beatrix Potter' to promote her hobbyhorses. For years she juggled the demands of her parents, the 'little books' and Hill Top; afterwards she separated Mrs Heelis's farming interests from Beatrix Potter's storytelling. The exception is *The Fairy Caravan*, written in the late 1920s for publication in the United States. Superficially concerned with a long-haired guinea pig and a magic fairy circus, this longer novel for older children showcases a number of Beatrix's concerns – protests against tree felling, tarmac roads and the replacement of horses by mechanised transport and machinery: 'this tarry asphalt like a level river of glass;... this treacherous granite where we toil and slip and stumble, dragged backward by our loads... Now it's rattle, rumble, rattle, rattle, shriek, shriek! Gone are the pleasant jog-trot days of peace. They have ruined the smithies and stolen the roads.'[9] An encomium on the fragile beauty of the Lakes and the changing face of farming provides the background to this picaresque story that Beatrix worried was too personal; her pen-and-ink illustrations included views of her farms.

In a letter written in February 1929 to Alexander McKay, the Philadelphia-based publisher of *The Fairy Caravan*, Beatrix referred to her 'picturesque farming'.[10] By the end of the year her landholdings exceeded 4,000 acres and included two flocks of Herdwick sheep, divided between low ground and the fells.

Her engagement with Herdwick sheep was the last of her naturalist's passions: as obsessive as her earlier absorption in insects, fungi or fossils. No longer able to paint as previously, she captured this love affair in words in *The Fairy Caravan*, which is partly a story of sheep; unusually, a sheep features among colour illustrations to *The Tale of Little Pig Robinson*, undertaken around the same time. But the attraction of Herdwicks to Beatrix was not as copy for her writing or her painting – like the bear she had sketched in the zoo for *The Tale of Timmy Tiptoes* or the Pomeranians on which she based Duchess. For Beatrix, Herdwicks symbolised a farming tradition and a way of life: she considered them living history. 'Sheep have been kept in this district from early times,' she told Henry P. Coolidge, the thirteen-year-old American boy with whom she formed an instant rapport when they met in Near Sawrey in 1927 and to whom she subsequently dedicated *The Fairy Caravan*. 'A fragment of woolen [*sic*] cloth was found in a "barrow" or ancient burial mound with a funeral urn, and bronze implements.'[11]

That Beatrix became a leading breeder of Herdwick sheep, the first woman elected president of the Herdwick Sheep Breeders' Association and, between 1930 and 1938, winner of every prize for Herdwick ewes at Keswick, Ennerdale, Eskdale and Loweswater shows,[12] came about as the result of two purchases: Troutbeck Park Farm with 1,875 acres, bought in 1923; and the larger Monk Coniston Farm, covering lengthy stretches of the Coniston and Tilberthwaite valleys, bought in 1929 in part with proceeds from *The Fairy Caravan*. In each case, Beatrix was drawn to the beauty of the landscape. Its silence and a tangible sense of venerable age appealed to her habit of quiet self-communing, the part of her that responded to a favourite rhyme: 'As I walked by myself, And talked by myself, Myself said unto me: Look to thyself, Take care of thyself, For nobody cares for thee.' Troutbeck Park Farm sits below the Kirkstone Pass, the mountain route that connects the Rothay and Ullswater valleys, in the shadow of a rock-scarred knoll known as Troutbeck Tongue; its fields stretch across the Tongue itself, to Ill Bell, Thornthwaite and Froswick. Beatrix described Troutbeck Tongue as 'uncanny; a place of silence and whispering echoes'. Her restoration of the seventeenth-century farmhouse included a study for herself. She employed a farm manager, Jimmy Hislop, and, for the large flock of Herdwick sheep she meant to rescue from its current 'rotten' state, a shepherd, Tom Storey. She lured Storey from a smaller farm nearby by doubling his wages. Five years later, with another pay rise, she moved him to Hill Top.

Alone she 'loved to wander on the Troutbeck Fell': she insisted she was never lonely. 'There was the company of gentle sheep, and wild flowers and singing waters', contentedly solitary experiences akin to some of the best moments of family holidays two decades before.[13] The country claimed her: open expanses of unspoilt North Country from which, she claimed, she traced her 'descent,... interests and... joy'. Her desire to safeguard its virgin tracts became evangelical; at a period of agricultural slump and in an area of expanding tourism, Beatrix understood their vulnerability.[14] With the 'little books' behind her, her focus had shifted. She balanced romance with common sense, and made plans from the outset to ensure the long-term survival of her new farms and age-old farming traditions by bequeathing both to the National Trust, a 'noble' institution, in Beatrix's eyes, associated with Hardwicke Rawnsley despite the day-to-day involvement of 'some silly mortals'. The Trust, she was convinced, offered the best possibilities of protecting the landscape she loved as working country.[15]

'There are great advantages to farm upon land under the Trust. The Trust, without income tax to pay and without death duties, can afford repairs and be a better landlord and give lasting security to good tenants.'[16]

Unlike the purchase of Hill Top or Castle Farm, Beatrix's large-scale later acquisitions were made with a specific intention of gifting the land to the National Trust after her death, and she altered her will in the immediate aftermath of her purchase of Troutbeck Park Farm in August 1923. Six years later, Beatrix bought Monk Coniston to guarantee its integrity. The £15,000 price tag was too much for the National Trust; it stretched Beatrix too and was only manageable after she sold the bulk of her investments. As soon as the Trust could raise the necessary funds, she offered it 2,600 acres at the price she had paid; she then set about fundraising vigorously on the Trust's behalf. She did not succeed in extracting a contribution from her mother. Beatrix's purchase of both estates represents an act of philanthropy worthy of her inherited traditions of Unitarianism and Victorian public-mindedness. At Monk Coniston, she also took on unpaid the management of all 3,738 acres, including the Trust's portion. By the time the Trust replaced Beatrix with a professional land agent in January 1937, Beatrix was months away from her seventy-first birthday. Predictably, this peppery and

determined woman was scathing in her assessment of
Bruce Thompson, the successor empowered to act with
the Trust's full authority and resources. She referred damn-
ingly to Thompson's 'blank' imagination; she regarded him
as 'supercilious' and 'deficient in experience'.[17]

From her first interest in Troutbeck Park Farm – alerted
by William of developers' plans to swallow up the rundown
acres – such all-consuming undertakings were a tall order
for a woman on the brink of her sixties, whose health had
been variable throughout her life, especially in the light of
her ingrained habits of 'thoroughness' and 'painstaking-
ness'. At once and in all weathers she set about familiarising
herself with every beck and field of her new possessions; in
1925, she embarked on a series of weekly letters to the new
secretary of the National Trust, Samuel Hamer. Still faithful to her statement of 1892 that 'the spirit of enquiry leads
up a lane which hath no ending', she revelled in the steep-
ness of her learning curve.[18] She ignored warning signs
that her health could not sustain such rigours: the colds
that confined her to bed, her continual fear of bronchitis,
bouts of sciatica, a feeling she likened to cold in her bones;
the weakness of her heart. She had embarked on what she
accurately labelled 'a labour of love... much scraping, and
hard work', the same combination of romantic optimism
and sturdy determination that had characterised all her

endeavours. Her 'declining years', she explained, would be devoted to 'old oak – and drains – and old roofs – and damp walls – oh the repairs!'[19] Although there was nothing disingenuous in her statement to Samuel Hamer in 1929 that she wanted 'neither praise nor thanks' for her efforts, her letters indicate her pride in 'hav[ing] tried to do my humble bit of preservation in this district'.[20] Her bequest to the National Trust at her death of more than 4,000 acres, including fifteen farms and an endowment of £5,000, is among the most significant Lake District donations in the Trust's history.

Her marriage to William Heelis had brought Beatrix companionship. With age her character betrayed signs of the obstinacy and indomitability which Jessy Potter had attributed to Crompton blood. Beatrix was unapologetic in her bluntness; she attributed William's later irritability to growing deafness. But their lives were harmonious, 'like two horses in front of the same plough... walk[ing] so steadily beside each other', like Amabella and Mr Tidler in *The Tale of the Faithful Dove*, 'a most devoted pair, after the habit of pigeons who marry for love'.[21] William's support buttressed Beatrix against the inevitable losses of passing time: the shock of Bertram's death, following long-term alcoholism, at the young age of forty-six in 1918; the less surprising demise, in May 1920, of Hardwicke Rawnsley; and, in December 1932, of the ninety-three-year-old Helen Potter. Beatrix was her mother's principal legatee; William was entrusted with the task of resolving death duties that exceeded £26,000. Beatrix wrote references for Helen Potter's servants and herself employed her mother's chauffeur.

'The stronger minded of the pair' was Beatrix's own estimation of her role in her marriage. Less conciliatory than William, decided in her views and confident in her financial independence, with 'the self-assurance of a person who is aware of the qualities within herself',[22] Beatrix gave the appearance to outsiders of dominating the Heelises' home life, but she was not a tartar; she likened herself to 'a good-tempered witch'.[23] 'I have acquiesced in such slovenly untidiness and unpunctuality' she wrote of their partnership towards the end of her life.[24] Not valuing appearances herself, busy and self-absorbed, Beatrix felt she had unfitted William to remarry after her death. She did not involve herself with his legal practice and, though she was proud to bear his name, she never defined herself principally as the wife of a country solicitor. She took pleasure in William's folk dancing, which inspired one of her last pieces of writing, 'The Lonely Hills', and she embraced his large, sometimes testing family to the extent of nursing his invalid brother Arthur, who lived at Castle Cottage with Beatrix and William from 1922 until his death four years later.

References to William in Beatrix's letters are characterised by the same warmth of feeling she reserved for favourite animals: Xarifa the dormouse, Peter and Benjamin, Mrs Tiggy, her black pig Sarah, the pair of Pekingese dogs, Tzusee and Chuleh – 'spirited and affectionate, and less trouble than terriers'[25] – who became the inseparable companions of her old age. Since she was not in the habit of unburdening herself emotionally in her letters, a special tenderness of tone amounted to high tribute.

Husband and wife spent evenings on the little tarn Beatrix had bought in 1913, William fishing, Beatrix beside him in the wooden boat; they gardened; at night Beatrix stoically endured William's heavy snoring. At the outbreak of the Second World War in 1939, William became the oldest reserve policeman in the area; Beatrix worried about him driving home late in the dark. Increasingly anxiety coloured her thoughts about William: like Beatrix he was tired and overworked. After a hysterectomy in 1939, Beatrix's main concern was for her husband: 'If it was not for poor W I would be indifferent to the result.'[26] Her last request, when, in December 1943, she lay dying, was to Hill Top's farm manager Tom Storey, that he 'manage the farm for Mr Heelis when she was gone'.[27] (She also made arrangements with Storey over the scattering of her ashes close to Hill Top, the exact location to be kept strictly secret.) Beatrix's anxiety proved well placed. William underwent a sharp decline after her death. He died less than eighteen months later, in August 1945, having occupied much of the intervening period with the ramifications of his late wife's estate.

Among William's tasks at Beatrix's death was replying to letters of condolence. A significant number came from the small group of American devotees who, beginning in 1921, had written to Beatrix and visited her in Near Sawrey. Although Beatrix delightedly described the States as a 'perfidiously complimentary nation', theirs were not ordinary fan letters.[28] Anne Carroll Moore, Superintendent of Children's Work at the New York Public Library; Bertha Mahony, co-founder of the Bookshop for Boys and Girls in Boston and an associated magazine about children's literature, *The Horn Book*; Marian Perry, a wealthy anglophile widow from Philadelphia; the Philadelphia publisher Alexander McKay of David McKay Co.; and Gail Templeman Coolidge, whose son Henry P. Coolidge partly inspired *The Fairy Caravan*, all shared an intense admiration for Beatrix's 'little books'. Their separate visits to Near Sawrey during the last two decades of Beatrix's life rekindled her confidence in her skills as a writer, beginning around the same time her relationship with Fruing Warne cooled. To Gail Templeman Coolidge, Beatrix wrote in December 1929, 'It has been a great pleasure to receive such kind *understanding* letters from you and others in America. And it is appreciation that is worth having. I feel that you take me seriously.'[29] Half a century earlier, Beatrix had resisted the influence of art teachers Miss Cameron and Mrs A.; she had withstood the scepticism of William Thiselton-Dyer and the Kew authorities; she had rebelled against her parents' dismissal of her stories and stubbornly fought to see the 'little books' in print, but no one since Norman had persuaded her of real value in her work. With their straightforward enthusiasm and generous, sincere praise, Beatrix's American admirers offered her a fillip she had long craved. That there were further Beatrix Potter books after *Cecily Parsley's Nursery Rhymes* was mostly their doing. Alexander McKay and Bertha Mahony coaxed Beatrix back into print; Anne Caroll Moore, Marian Perry and Gail Templeman Coolidge convinced her the effort was worth making.

Referring to herself in the third person, Beatrix described herself in 1925 as living 'amongst the mountains and lakes that she has drawn in her picture books... She leads a very busy contented life, living always in the country and managing a large sheep farm on her own land.'[30] Her shepherd Tom Storey described her as 'quite smart for her age... a bonny looking woman', robust at the start of her seventh decade.[31] Ten years later, with 'apple-red' cheeks and blue eyes undimmed, she appeared 'short, plump, solid', to artist Delmar Banner, who painted Beatrix's best-known portrait – a tweedy Mrs Tiggy-winkle figure at a sheep judging on the Coniston fells.[32] Other observers noted marked eccentricities of dress: 'the sacking she put over her shoulders in the rain', 'the use of a rhubarb leaf on her head against the sun in the hayfield'.[33] Much to her amusement, a tramp on the Windermere ferry mistook Beatrix for a fellow vagrant. She dressed as she thought practical for a life spent in the fields, walking and watching. Banner described 'a kind of tea cosy' on her head and 'lots of wool' clothes.

Beatrix recognised the vagaries of her health. She understood that the life she led would inevitably exact its toll, but she had 'no wish to give in and live as an invalide [sic]'.[34] Over time, battered by the local climate and, beginning in 1939, three consecutive hard winters which troubled her chest and her heart, she oscillated between resignation to her own mortality and a stubborn desire to carry on. She had described the general anaesthetic necessitated by her hysterectomy in 1939 as 'such a wonderfully easy going under; and in some ways preferable to a long invalidism, with only old age to follow'.[35] Crompton pluck brought her back from the brink and kept her busy; she remained assiduous in overseeing her scattered property and still interested in the breeding programmes she had set in train years ago for Herdwick sheep and Galloway cattle. 'Even on unsuitable occasions' she remained mostly cheerful, 'doomed to go through life *grinning!*'[36] The resource she had always treasured, her memory, was sharp still, its balm 'like soft music and a blissful vision through the snow'.[37] She dealt with pain briskly; she accepted without self-pity the malignity of old age.

From the second half of the 1930s she was repeatedly confined to bed, Tzusee and Chuleh useful foot warmers in the winter chill of Castle Cottage. When she closed her eyes at these moments, she wrote to her cousin Caroline, she found she could 'walk step by step on the fells and rough lands seeing every stone and flower and patch of bog cotton grass where my old legs will never take me again.'[38] During her final illness, after months of bronchitis, her thoughts retrod the familiar paths – divided between her farms, her family, with its far-flung network of cousins and cousins' children, and a last story she had written,

218

scheduled for publication in May 1944 in the twentieth anniversary issue of *The Horn Book*: 'Wag-by-Wall', about an old woman and a kettle, begun decades earlier. Beatrix died six months short of publication, on 22 December 1943: she never read 'Wag-by-Wall' in print. William was at her bedside, the last person she saw.

Her instructions for the disposal of her property were characteristically precise and extended, inevitably, to animals: 'No old horse or worn out dog to be sold; either given to a really trustworthy person or put down.'[39] No detail was too small for firm, clear instructions; she allocated paintings and portfolios with care; she had made her arrangements with the National Trust. Among her final requests was that a 'looking glass... and the small chest of drawers which it stands on' be moved from Castle Cottage to Hill Top. Today they occupy a place beside the window in Hill Top's upstairs sitting room, with its view over Beatrix's first garden.

In the near distance lies another garden, the 'regular old-fashioned farm garden' Beatrix made at Castle Cottage, 'with a box hedge round the flower bed, and moss rose and pansies and black currants and strawberries and peas – and big sage bushes for Jemima.'[40] In summer, when both houses are 'nearly smothered with roses'[41] – often, as Beatrix experienced them, weighed down with rain over the porch or the door – the outlook is intensely green. It stretches up and down the rises and inclines of Near Sawrey; it stretches to the secret spot above Hill Top where William and Tom Storey scattered Beatrix's ashes; it stretches beyond, past stone cottages and snaking lanes to wooded copses and the blue slopes of mountains and the distant glimmer of sunlight on lake water, over the hills and far away.

'Little friends of Mr McGregor & Peter & Benjamin'

'"That story," said Pony Billy, "has no moral."
"But it is very pretty," said Xarifa,
the dormouse, suddenly waking up'

The Fairy Caravan, 1929

IT IS 31 JULY 2009, North Wales, a summer evening of a middling sort, blue-grey light stretching across the folded hills of the Clwydian Range, smudging the shadows of trees, pooling in hollows of banks and rises. At Gwaenynog, the 'Gwaynynog' of Beatrix's letters and journal, Beatrix Potter's great-niece Janey Smith, the great-granddaughter of Harriet Leech and her husband Fred Burton, has put on an apron and mob cap.

In the little theatre that stands at right angles to the house, chair legs shuffle over wooden floorboards. Many of the audience know one another. They have gathered (some by invitation) to watch a performance of *The Tale of the Flopsy Bunnies*. Snatches of conversation spill through the open theatre door across the yard choked by cars, over the garden Beatrix would still recognise: 'two-thirds surrounded by a red brick wall with many apricots, and an inner circle of old grey apple trees on wooden espaliers... productive but not tidy, the prettiest kind of garden, where bright old-fashioned flowers grow amongst the currant bushes', 'cauliflowers [are] mixed with peonies & roses' and there are 'white and damask roses, and the smell of thyme and musk'.[1]

It is the same garden that inspired the story of the Flopsy Bunnies, first published a century ago, and Beatrix's own garden at Hill Top; and the evening will end – to the considerable surprise of some – with the audience singing 'Happy Birthday, Flopsy Bunnies'.

On this occasion, most of the 'actors' are children, Janey Smith's grandchildren, each linked to Beatrix Potter by a dribble of consanguinity, and my own son, Aeneas, just five, then living outside the neighbouring village of Nantglyn, probably the hillside hamlet Beatrix described to Noel Moore in 1895 as 'a nasty dirty Welsh village'.[2] The children are dressed as Flopsy Bunnies in brown leggings. In nearby Denbigh, Woolworths – soon to disappear from the British high street – has supplied hairbands with large brown rabbit ears. When the moment comes, the children's responses to incarceration in Mr McGregor's sack will vary, adding an inadvertent note of comedy. Potter scholar and biographer Judy Taylor has spent the day at Gwaenynog; so, too, actress Rohan McCullough, who has recently toured the country with her one-woman show, *The Tale of Beatrix Potter*, and will narrate tonight's performance. Janey plays the part of Mrs McGregor.

At curtain down, each child receives a copy of *The Tale of the Flopsy Bunnies* in a special gold centenary dust jacket. Beatrix dedicated her story to 'all little friends of Mr McGregor & Peter & Benjamin': admission to a golden circle. Aeneas's copy stands on a bookcase in his bedroom, alongside Potter's other 'little books'.

As a young woman Beatrix Potter wrote in her journal, 'There is something rather mournful in people dying without children, complete extinction.'[3] It has not been her own fate, as that evening at Gwaenynog proved, despite her childlessness. With satisfaction, she could claim of Peter Rabbit at the end of her life, 'his moderate price has at least enabled him to reach many hundreds of thousands of children, and has given them pleasure without ugliness'.[4] Since first publication in 1902, Peter's story has sold more than 40 million copies worldwide; a recent estimate suggested that, somewhere in the world, one of Beatrix's 'little books' is purchased every fifteen seconds. The appeal of Potter's stories is perennial and the circle of 'little friends of Mr McGregor & Peter & Benjamin' continually replenished.

She was fascinated by the childhood narratives of fairy tales and traditional rhymes and, in lesser measure, her own childhood; her relish of poetic narrative was anchored by a solidly practical streak. Her love of nature was aesthetic, scientific, empathetic, *obsessive*; capable of embracing everything from the 'white scented funguses' she found in a wood on a Highland hillside to the sure-footed Herdwick sheep which 'heafed' themselves to upland fell pastures. 'I see no reason why common-sense should not foster a healthier appreciation of beauty than morbid sentimentality,' she wrote once; common sense underpinned her own endeavours, from management of the 'little books' and their lucrative 'side-shows' to her stewardship of her Lake District farms.[5] She did not discount whimsy, but balanced it with sharply ironic humour – and not only within the tales. That she described herself as one of the 'children-who-have-never-grown-up' was an aspiration as much as an assessment.[6]

As Unitarians the Potters readily assimilated Darwinism and its body blow to the doctrine of creationism. The relationship between humans and animals in nineteenth-century evolutionary theories adds an extra dimension to the anthropomorphism of Beatrix's stories, in different instances reassuring or unsettling. As a farmer, she loved, feared and respected nature in equal measure.

Beatrix described herself once as in thrall to fancies so real she could not distinguish between fact and imagining. She did not always attempt to do so and her best work emerged from a blurring of fancy and close observation. The vividness of her childhood drawings of a devil kept her awake at night: credibility was key to the success of all her work. On the printed page hers is simultaneously a vision of its time – offering a critique of contemporary mores through the harmless-seeming vehicle of talking animals, and shaped by Victorian conservatism as well as her unabashed joy in the world she depicted – and timeless in its sheer improbability and the repeated reinvention of the age-old trope of children versus adults. Beatrix's work on the 'little books' was painstaking: 'I like to do my work carefully,' she wrote.[7] Her husbandry of animals and the land betrayed the same conscientiousness. And she had confidence in her efforts. She told the Danish wife of a cousin's son: 'You share your nationality with Hans Christian Andersen. I tell you... my children's stories will one day be as famous and as much read as his.'[8] At Hill Top she correctly anticipated posterity's verdict and created a museum to her own imaginings.

Unlike much Edwardian literature, Potter's tales have escaped the coruscation of revisionist social, sexual and racial politics. To sing 'Happy Birthday, Flopsy Bunnies' in a private theatre at the end of a winding wooded drive amid the still-unspoiled upland fields of North Wales is, of course, a self-conscious act. But it is not impossible. It is just one measure of the extent to which Beatrix Potter, who married much too late for childbearing, defies extinction – and continues to beguile new generations of 'little friends' with her vision of nature improved but not perfected.

Author's Note

For help and information I should very much like to thank
Libby Joy and Mandy Marshall of the Beatrix Potter Society
and Sue Osman of the Armitt Museum and Library. Judy
Taylor Hough, doyenne of Potter scholars, offered support
and encouragement. My former neighbour Janey Smith is
among several custodians of Potter's memory, a task she
embraces with sincerity and lightness of touch.

My chief debt is to Linda Lear, author of *Beatrix Potter:*
A Life in Nature, whose boundless generosity of spirit and
helpful advice, dispensed unstintingly from Washington
and Connecticut, provided a matchless fillip during the
writing of this book.

I should like to thank Anthony Cheetham, Richard
Milbank and Georgina Blackwell of Head of Zeus, and
my exceptional agent, Georgina Capel, of Georgina Capel
Associates.

As ever, my wonderful wife Gráinne showed extraordinary forbearance during the writing of this account

of Potter's life. Nor did my parents, Michael and Jane Dennison, object to a landmark birthday being hijacked for yet another Lake District sojourn.

This book is dedicated to my adored son Aeneas, at whose bedside I rediscovered Potter's genius.

Matthew Dennison Montgomeryshire,

Trinity Sunday, 2017

Bibliography

Battrick, Elizabeth, *The Real World of Beatrix Potter* (National Trust and Jarrold Publishing, Norwich, 1987)

Beatrix Potter Studies I–XIV (The Beatrix Potter Society, London, 1984–2010)

Carpenter, Humphrey, *Secret Gardens: A Study of the Golden Age of Children's Literature* (Allen & Unwin, London, 1985)

Crowell Morse, Jane, ed., *Beatrix Potter's Americans: Selected Letters* (Horn Book, Boston, 1982)

Davies, Hunter, *Beatrix Potter's Lakeland* (Frederick Warne, London, 1988)

Denyer, Susan, *Beatrix Potter: At Home in the Lake District* (Frances Lincoln, London, 2000)

de Vasconcelles, Josefina, *She was Loved: Memories of Beatrix Potter* (Titus Wilson, Kendal, 2003)

Gere, Charlotte, *Artistic Circles: Design & Decoration in the Aesthetic Movement* (V&A Publishing, London, 2010)

Haining, Peter, *Movable Books* (New English Library, London, 1979)

Heelis, John, *The Tale of Mrs William Heelis – Beatrix Potter* (Sutton Publishing, 1999)

Hyde Parker, Ulla, *Cousin Beatie: A Memory of Beatrix Potter* (Frederick Warne, London, 1981)

Jay, Eileen, Noble, Mary and Hobbs, Anne Stevenson, *A Victorian*

Naturalist: Beatrix Potter's Drawings from the Armitt Collection (Frederick Warne, London, 1992)

Lane, Margaret, *The Tale of Beatrix Potter* (Frederick Warne, London, 1946, repr 1985)

— *The Magic Years of Beatrix Potter* (Frederick Warne, London, 1978)

Lear, Linda, *Beatrix Potter: A Life in Nature* (Allen Lane, London, 2007)

Linder, Leslie, *The Journal of Beatrix Potter, From 1881 to 1897*, transcribed from her code writings (Frederick Warne, London 1966; revised edition, 1989)

— *A History of the Writings of Beatrix Potter, including Unpublished Work* (Frederick Warne, London, 1971)

Linder, Leslie & Enid, *The Art of Beatrix Potter* (Frederick Warne, London, 1975)

McDowell, Marta, *Beatrix Potter's Gardening Life* (Timber Press, Portland, Oregon, 2013)

Norman, Andrew, *Beatrix Potter Her Inner World* (Pen & Sword Books, Barnsley, 2014)

Price, John, *Everyday Heroism: Victorian Constructions of the Victorian Civilian* (Bloomsbury Academic, London, 2014)

Sheppard, F. W. H., ed., *Survey of London, vol. 41, Brompton*, ed. (London County Council, London, 1983)

Stevenson Hobbs, Anne, *Beatrix Potter Artist & Illustrator* (Frederick Warne, London, 2005)

Taylor, Judy, intro., *Beatrix Potter's Letters* (Frederick Warne, London, 1989)

Taylor, Judy, *Beatrix Potter: Artist, Storyteller and Countrywoman* (Frederick Warne, London, 1986)

— *Beatrix Potter and Hill Top* (National Trust, London, 1989)

Taylor, Judy, ed., *Letters to Children from Beatrix Potter* (Frederick Warne, London, 1992)

— *The Choyce Letters* (The Beatrix Potter Society, London, 1994)

— *Beatrix Potter: A Holiday Diary* (The Beatrix Potter Society, London, 1996)

— *Beatrix Potter's Farming Friendship: Lake District Letters to Joseph Moscrop, 1926–1943* (The Beatrix Potter Society, London, 1998)

Taylor, Judy, Whalley, Joyce Irene, et al., *Beatrix Potter 1866–1943: The Artist and Her World* (Frederick Warne with the National Trust, London, 1987)

Wood, Christopher, *Fairies in Victorian Art* (Antique Collectors' Club, Woodbridge, 2000)

Notes

The Journal of Beatrix Potter is referred to as BPJ after first listing; *Beatrix Potter's Letters*, BPL after first listing.

Chapter 1

1 Beatrix Potter, *The Journal of Beatrix Potter, From 1881 to 1897*, transcribed from her code writings by Leslie Linder (Frederick Warne & Co., London 1966; revised edition, 1989), May 1890, p. 212.

2 BPJ, 12 October 1892, p. 289; Beatrix Potter to Norman Warne, 22 May 1902, *Beatrix Potter's Letters*, selected and introduced by Judy Taylor (Frederick Warne & Co., London, 1989), p. 62.

3 BPJ, 8 February 1884, p. 67.

4 Beatrix Potter to Eleanor Rawnsley, 21 October 1934, BPL, p. 366.

5 *Survey of London, vol. 41, Brompton*, ed. F. H. W. Sheppard (London County Council, London, 1983), pp. 195–202.

6 BPJ, 31 October 1882, p. 25.

7 BPJ, 30 January 1884, p. 67.

8 BPJ, 23 April 1883, p. 39.

9 BPJ, 28 July 1892, p. 248.

10 Beatrix Potter to Norman Warne, 20 April 1904, BPL, p. 93.

11 Collins, Wilkie, *The Woman in White* (repr Penguin Classics, London, 2003), p. 483.

12 Beatrix Potter to Sylvie Heelis, 17 September 1921, BPL, p. 272; and Beatrix Potter to John Stone, 5 June 1940, BPL, p. 416.

13 BPJ, 31 October 1882, p. 25.

14 Beatrix Potter to Louie Choyce, 2 May 1923, *The Choyce Letters*, ed. Judy Taylor (The Beatrix Potter Society, London, 1994), p. 26.

15 *Beatrix Potter's Americans: Selected Letters*, ed. Jane Crowell Morse (Horn Book, Boston, 1982), p. 213.

16 BPJ, 19 May 1884, p. 87; 9 October 1885, p. 158.

17 BPJ, 19 May 1883, p. 46.

18 Lane, Margaret, *The Tale of Beatrix Potter* (Frederick Warne & Co., London, 1946, repr 1985), p. 46.

19 *Beatrix Potter's Americans*, p. 208.

20 Taylor, Judy, *Beatrix Potter: Artist, Storyteller and Countrywoman* (Frederick Warne & Co., London, 1986), p. 20.

21 Potter, Beatrix, *The Fairy Caravan* (Frederick Warne & Co., London, 1929, repr 1986), p. 83.

22 BPJ, 16 July 1884, p. 100.

23 Beatrix Potter to Marian Frazer Harris Perry, 4 October 1934, BPL, p. 365; Lear, Linda, *Beatrix Potter: A Life in Nature* (Allen Lane, London, 2007), p. 37.

24 BPJ, 3 March 1883, p. 32.

25 BPJ, 3 November 1885, p. 159.

26 BPJ, 19 July 1884, p. 102; BPJ, 12 February 1886, p. 182.

27 BPJ, 29 August 1894, p. 341.

28 BPJ, 7 September 1885, p. 156.

29 Beatrix Potter to Norman Warne, 18 February 1904, BPL, p. 86.

30 Potter, Beatrix, *Memories of Camfield Place* (c.1891), BPJ, p. 446.

31 Roberts, Ronald, 'The "cross old nurse"', *The Beatrix Potter Society Journal and Newsletter* 136 (April 2015), p. 15.

32 BPJ, 5 June 1891, p. 215.

33 Lane, Margaret, op. cit., p. 31.

34 Carpenter, Humphrey, *Secret Gardens: A Study of the Golden Age of Children's Literature* (Allen & Unwin, London, 1985), p. 143.

35 BPJ, 14 December 1895, p. 411.

36 Beatrix Potter to Bertha Mahony Miller, 25 November 1940, BPL, p. 423.

37 Beatrix Potter, 20 August 1905, *Beatrix Potter: A Holiday Diary*, ed. Judy Taylor (The Beatrix Potter Society, London, 1996), pp. 49–50.

38 *Memories of Camfield Place*, BPJ, p. 448.

39 Taylor, Judy, Whalley, Joyce Irene, et al., *Beatrix Potter 1866–1943: The Artist and Her World* (Frederick Warne & Co. with the National Trust, London, 1987), p. 61.

40 See *The Tale of the Faithful Dove*, p. 11.

41 Beatrix Potter to Henry P. Coolidge, see *Letters to Children from Beatrix Potter* (Frederick Warne & Co., London, 1992), collected and introduced by Judy Taylor, p. 213.

42 Taylor, Judy, op. cit. (BP: A, S & C), p. 82.

43 *Memories of Camfield Place*, BPJ, p. 446.

44 Beatrix Potter to Sylvie Heelis, 17 September 1921, BPL, p. 272.

45 Beatrix Potter to Caroline Clark, 19 December 1933, BPL, p. 360.

46 Beatrix Potter to Marian Frazer Harris Perry, 4 October 1934, BPL, p. 365.

CHAPTER 2

1 BPJ, 19 March 1884, p. 76.

2 Norman, Andrew, *Beatrix Potter Her Inner World* (Pen & Sword Books, Barnsley, 2014), p. 24.

3 BPJ, 5 June 1891, p. 216.

4 BPJ, 19 January 1884, p. 63.

5 Haining, Peter, *Movable Books* (New English Library, London, 1979), pp. 30-31.

6 Beatrix Potter to Harold Warne, 20 November 1911, BPL, p. 189; Lane, Margaret, *The Tale of Beatrix Potter* (Frederick Warne & Co., London, 1946, repr 1985), p. 65.

7 Beatrix Potter to Helen Dean Fish, 8 December 1934, BPL, p. 369; Taylor, Judy, Whalley, Joyce Irene, et al., *Beatrix Potter 1866-1943: The Artist and Her World* (Frederick Warne & Co. with the National Trust, London, 1987), p. 45.

8 Taylor, Judy, *Beatrix Potter: Artist, Storyteller and Countrywoman* (Frederick Warne & Co., London, 1986), p. 19.

9 Molesworth, Mary Louisa ('Mrs'), *The Cuckoo Clock* (1877), see Chapter 5.

10 BPJ, 11 October 1895.

11 Beatrix Potter to Marjorie Moore, 13 March 1900, *Letters to Children from Beatrix Potter* (Frederick Warne & Co., London, 1992), collected and introduced by Judy Taylor, p. 66.

12 Carpenter, Humphrey, *Secret Gardens: A Study of the Golden Age of Children's Literature* (Allen & Unwin, London, 1985), p. 143.

13 Beatrix Potter to Harold Warne, 20 August 1909, BPL, p. 170.

14 Beatrix Potter to Marian Frazer Harris Perry, 4 October 1934, BPL, p. 365.

15 Hyde Parker, Ulla, *Cousin Beatie: A Memory of Beatrix Potter* (Frederick Warne & Co., London, 1981), p. 21.

16 Beatrix Potter to Mrs Ramsay Duff, 13 July 1943, *Beatrix Potter's Americans: Selected Letters*, ed. Jane Crowell Morse (Horn Book, Boston, 1982).

17 BPJ, 10 September 1895, p. 401.

18 Taylor, Judy, (BP A S &C) op. cit., p. 21; BPJ, 19 May 1884, p. 87.

19 BPJ, 9 April 1895, p. 374.

20 BPJ, 8 May 1884, p. 85.

21 BPJ, 12 September 1892, p. 267.

22 Taylor, Judy, op. cit., p. 25.

23 Carpenter, Humphrey, op. cit., p. 141.

24 BPJ, 17 March 1893, p. 317.

25 BPJ, 31 March 1892, p. 221.

26 BPJ, 8 May 1884, p. 85.

27 Lear, Linda, *Beatrix Potter: A Life in Nature* (Allen Lane, London, 2007), p. 279.

28 BPJ, 14 June 1884, p. 94.

29 Taylor, Whalley, et al., op. cit., p. 79; BPJ, 28 July 1896, p. 427.

30 BPJ, 28 March 1884, p. 79; BPJ, 17 November 1896, p. 435.

31 Beatrix Potter to Lady Warren, 23 December 1919, BPL, p. 260.

32 *Memories of Camfield Place*, BPJ, p. 447.

33 Ibid.

34 BPJ, December 1886, p. 201.

35 *Memories of Camfield Place*, BPJ, p. 448.

36 Potter, Beatrix, *The Fairy Caravan* (Frederick Warne & Co., London, 1929, repr 1986), p. 53.

37 Beatrix Potter to Mr D. M. Matheson, 17 October 1939, BPL, p. 410.

38 *Memories of Camfield Place*, BPJ, p. 444.

39 Taylor, Judy, op. cit., p. 28.

40 BPJ, 19 February 1885, p. 131.

41 *Memories of Camfield Place*, BPJ, p. 444.

42 BPJ, 28 May 1895, p. 384.

43 BPJ, 11 November 1884, p. 115.

44 BPJ, 2 July 1884, p. 96.

45 BPJ, 23 February 1886, p. 188.

46 Beatrix Potter to Caroline Clark, 15 February 1937, BPL, p. 384.

47 Beatrix Potter to Henry P. Coolidge, 27 October 1929, BPL, p. 322.

48   BPJ, late May 1887, p. 204.

49   BPJ, 10 July 1885; Beatrix Potter to Fruing Warne, 28 February
     1919, BPL, p. 254

50   Beatrix Potter to Denys Lowson, 3 October 1916, BPL, p. 228.

51   BPJ, 28 May 1883, p. 47.

52   BPJ, 4 October 1884, p. 109.

CHAPTER 3

1   BPJ, 10 June 1882, pp. 17–19.

2   Taylor, Judy, Whalley, Joyce Irene, et al., *Beatrix Potter
     1866–1943: The Artist and Her World* (Frederick Warne & Co.
     with the National Trust, London, 1987), p. 74.

3   BPJ, 2 August 1883, p. 50.

4   Ibid., p. 51.

5   Lear, Linda, *Beatrix Potter: A Life in Nature* (Allen Lane,
     London, 2007), p. 371.

6   Beatrix Potter to Fruing Warne, 5 August 1921, BPL, p. 271;
     Beatrix Potter to Sylvie Heelis, 17 September 1921, BPL, p. 273.

7   Beatrix Potter to Sylvie Heelis, 17 September 1921, BPL, p. 273.

8   BPJ, 28 July 1883, p. 49.

9   BPJ, 19 May 1883, p. 46.

10   BPJ, 18 October 1892, p. 295.

11   BPJ, 24 August 1895, p. 398.

12   Lane, Margaret, *The Tale of Beatrix Potter* (Frederick Warne &
     Co., London, 1946, repr 1985), p. 40; Beatrix Potter to Norman
     Warne, 2 November 1904, BPL, p. 106.

13   Taylor, Whalley, op. cit., p. 92.

14   BPJ, June 1894, p. 319.

15   Beatrix Potter to Norman Warne, 7 December 1904, BPL,
     p. 110.

16   BPJ, 2 May 1883, p. 44.

17 BPJ, 7 March 1886, p. 192.

18 Ibid.

19 Beatrix Potter to Arthur Stephens, 7 February 1943, BPL,
    p. 455; Beatrix Potter to Janet Adam Smith, 8 February 1943,
    BPL, p. 456; Beatrix Potter to Millie Warne, 13 December 1911,
    BPL, p. 192.

20 BPJ, 3 April 1886, p. 196.

21 Beatrix Potter to Sylvie Heelis, 17 September 1921, BPL, p. 272.

22 BPJ, 30 January 1884, p. 66.

23 Beatrix Potter to Elizabeth Hadfield, 28 January 1910, BPL,
    p. 184.

24 Beatrix Potter to Eileen Rowson, 6 March 1919, BPL, p. 256.

25 BPJ, 7 March 1886, p. 193.

26 Taylor, Whalley, op. cit., p. 79.

27 BPJ, 19 November 1884, p. 117.

28 BPJ, 9 February 1884, p. 68.

29 Lane, Margaret, op. cit., p. 45.

30 Taylor, Whalley, op. cit., p. 77.

31 Beatrix Potter, draft letter to newspaper (unpublished),
    November 1911, BPL, p. 191.

32 BPJ, 20 September 1883, p. 54.

33 Taylor, Whalley, op. cit., p. 77.

34 Ibid., p. 69.

35 BPJ, 8 December 1883, p. 59.

36 Beatrix Potter to Eileen Rowson, 6 March 1919, BPL, p. 255.

37 Beatrix Potter to Norman Warne, 12 November 1904, BPL,
    p. 107.

38 Beatrix Potter to Eileen Rowson, 6 March 1919, BPL, p. 255.

39 Lane, Margaret, op. cit., p. 51.

40 Beatrix Potter to Miss Wyatt, 27 November 1920, BPL, p. 266.

41 Ibid.

42 Beatrix Potter to William Warner, 11 August 1908, private collection.

43 BPJ, December 1886, p. 202.

44 Potter, Beatrix, *The Fairy Caravan* (Frederick Warne & Co., London, 1929, repr 1986), p. 28.

45 Beatrix Potter to 'Dulcie', 16 November 1923, *Letters to Children from Beatrix Potter* (Frederick Warne & Co., London, 1992), collected and introduced by Judy Taylor, p. 182.

46 Beatrix Potter to Mrs M. C. Grimston, 12 February 1938, BPL, p. 386.

47 BPJ, May 1890, p. 212.

48 Beatrix Potter to Mrs M. C. Grimston, 12 February 1938, BPL, p. 386.

49 Ibid.

50 Taylor, Whalley, et al., op. cit., p. 96.

51 Beatrix Potter to Bertha Mahony Miller, 25 November 1940, BPL, p. 422.

52 Beatrix Potter to Walter Gaddum, 6 March 1897, *Letters to Children from Beatrix Potter*, op. cit., p. 100.

53 Lane, Margaret, op. cit., p. 50.

54 Taylor, Judy, *Beatrix Potter: Artist, Storyteller and Countrywoman* (Frederick Warne & Co., London, 1986), p. 80.

55 Taylor, Whalley, et al., op. cit., p. 77.

56 Lane, Margaret, op. cit., p. 50.

57 Ibid.

58 Beatrix Potter, *The Tale of Little Pig Robinson*, p. 84.

59 Taylor, Whalley, et al., op. cit., p. 71.

60 Ibid., p. 77.

61 BPJ, 20 April 1884, p. 82.

62 BPJ, 10 July 1885, p. 154.

63 BPJ, 8 May 1884, p. 85.

64 BPJ, May 1890, p. 213.

65 Beatrix Potter to Noel Moore, 4 February 1895, *Letters to Children*, op. cit., p. 28.

66 BPJ, 26 July 1892, p. 246; see packing list, BPJ, March 1889, p. 209.

67 Hyde Parker, Ulla, *Cousin Beatie: A Memory of Beatrix Potter* (Frederick Warne & Co., London, 1981), p. 7.

68 Lane, Margaret, op. cit., p. 38.

69 Beatrix Potter to Norman Warne, 12 February 1904, BPL, p. 85.

70 BPJ, 21 July 1882, p. 21.

71 Beatrix Potter to Norman Warne, ?September 1903, BPL, p. 81; see also Beatrix Potter to Norman Warne, 20 October 1904, BPL, p. 104.

72 Beatrix Potter to Louie Choyce, 17 September 1943, *The Choyce Letters*, ed. Judy Taylor (The Beatrix Potter Society, London, 1994), p. 75.

73 BPJ, 10 June 1884, p. 93.

74 BPJ, 21 July 1882, p. 20.

75 BPJ, 8 May 1884, p. 84.

76 BPJ, 19 May 1884, p. 87.

77 BPJ, 27 May 1884, p. 89.

CHAPTER 4

1 BPJ, December 1886, p. 201.

2 BPJ, April to May 1887, pp. 203–204.

3 BPJ, 18 August 1896, p. 429.

4 BPJ, 22 February 1883, p. 31.

5 BPJ, late December 1883, p. 61.

6 BPJ, 21 to 25 May 1883, p. 47.

7 BPJ, 29 April 1884, p. 83.

8 Caroline Clark (née Hutton), 1956, quoted in BPJ, p. 319n.

9   BPJ, 6 May 1885, p. 146.
10 BPJ, 28 March 1885, pp. 143-4; 7 September 1885, p. 156.
11 BPJ, 28 March 1885, p. 143.
12 BPJ, 29 May 1885, p. 149.
13 BPJ, p. xvii.
14 BPJ, 22 February 1884, p. 71.
15 BPJ, 12 October 1884, p. 109.
16 BPJ, 8 August 1883, p. 51.
17 BPJ, June 1894, p. 321.
18 BPJ, 30 April 1883, p. 43.
19 BPJ, 10 June 1882, p. 18.
20 BPJ, 19 March 1884, p. 78.
21 Ibid., p. 77.
22 BPJ, 7 September 1885, p. 156.
23 BPJ, 13 October 1885, p. 158.
24 BPJ, 7 September 1885, p. 156.
25 BPJ, 25 April 1883, p. 39.
26 Ibid.
27 Ibid.
28 Ibid.
29 Beatrix Potter to Norman Warne, 22 May 1902, BPL, p. 62.
30 BPJ, May 1890, p. 212.
31 BPJ, 24 April 1884, p. 83.
32 BPJ, 9 November 1885, p. 160.
33 BPJ, May 1890, p. 213.
34 BPJ, 6 November 1894, p. 365.
35 Beatrix Potter to Freda Moore, 14 June 1897, BPL, p. 43.
36 Lear, Linda, *Beatrix Potter: A Life in Nature* (Allen Lane, London, 2007), p. 442.
37 BPJ, 28 July 1883, p. 49.
38 Lear, Linda, op. cit., p. 136.

39 BPJ, 13 December 1884, p. 122.

40 BPJ, 24 November 1883, p. 58.

41 BPJ, 29 April 1884, p. 83.

42 BPJ, 25 June 1884, p. 94.

43 BPJ, 28 November 1884, p. 120.

44 BPJ, 4 October 1884, p. 109.

45 Ibid.

46 BPJ, 28 November 1884, p. 121.

47 BPJ, 21 November 1883, p. 57.

48 BPJ, 24 November 1883, p. 58.

49 BPJ, 27 October 1884, p. 110.

50 BPJ, 14 March 1884, p. 74.

51 BPJ, 28 May 1883, p. 47.

52 BPJ, 31 December 1885, p. 168.

53 BPJ, April 1892, p. 244.

54 BPJ, May 1890, p. 212.

55 BPJ, May 1890, p. 214.

56 Lear, Linda, op. cit., p. 74.

Chapter 5

1 Beatrix Potter to Noel Moore, 4 September 1893, BPL, p. 26.

2 Beatrix Potter to Bertha Mahony Miller, 25 November 1940, BPL, p. 422.

3 BPJ, 21 August 1892, pp. 256-7.

4 Beatrix Potter to Janet Adam Smith, 8 February 1943, BPL, p. 456.

5 Beatrix Potter to Josephine Banner, 28 February 1938, BPL, p. 387.

6 Beatrix Potter to Bertha Mahony Miller, 25 November 1940, BPL, p. 423.

7   Beatrix Potter to Marian Frazer Harris Perry, 4 October 1934,
     BPL, p. 365.

8   BPJ, 19 February 1885, p. 131.

9   BPJ, 29 July 1894, p. 330.

10   Beatrix Potter to Bertha Mahony Miller, 25 November 1940,
     BPL, p. 422.

11   BPJ, 11 November 1895, p. 409.

12   BPJ, 3 October 1892, p. 278.

13   BPJ, 20 August 1896, p. 430.

14   BPJ, 17 November 1896, p. 435.

15   BPJ, mid-April 1896, p. 421.

16   BPJ, 10 October 1894, p. 364.

17   Linder, Leslie & Enid, *The Art of Beatrix Potter* (Frederick
     Warne & Co., London, 1975), p. 274.

18   BPJ, 25 September 1894, p. 354.

19   Beatrix Potter to Walter Gaddum, 6 March 1897, *Letters to
     Children from Beatrix Potter* (Frederick Warne & Co., London,
     1992), collected and introduced by Judy Taylor, p. 100.

20   BPJ, 18 August 1894, p. 337.

21   BPJ, 23 July 1896, p. 426.

22   BPJ, 18 August 1894, pp. 337–8.

23   Taylor, Judy, Whalley, Joyce Irene, et al., *Beatrix Potter
     1866–1943: The Artist and Her World* (Frederick Warne & Co.
     with the National Trust, London, 1987), p. 91.

24   BPJ, 2 October 1894, p. 357.

25   BPJ, 29 October 1892, p. 306.

26   Ibid., p. 305.

27   Lear, Linda, *Beatrix Potter: A Life in Nature* (Allen Lane,
     London, 2007), p. 87.

28   Beatrix Potter to Charles McIntosh, 10 December 1892, BPL,
     p. 18.

29 Beatrix Potter to Charles McIntosh, ?1893, BPL, p. 19.

30 Beatrix Potter to Walter Gaddum, 6 March 1897, *Letters to Children*, op. cit., p. 100.

31 Beatrix Potter to Charles McIntosh, 12 January 1897, BPL, p. 39.

32 BPJ, 7 December 1896, p. 438.

33 Ibid.

34 BPJ, 11 December 1896, p. 439; also see BPJ, entries January 9 to 31, 1897, pp. 441–443.

35 Price, John, *Everyday Heroism: Victorian Constructions of the Victorian Civilian* (Bloomsbury Academic, London, 2014), p. 86.

36 Ibid., p. 85.

37 Beatrix Potter to Norman Warne, 14 February 1905, BPL, p. 113.

38 Beatrix Potter to Messrs Warne & Co., 11 September 1901, BPL, p. 55.

39 Lear, Linda, op. cit., p. 136.

40 Ibid., p. 150.

41 Lane, Margaret, *The Tale of Beatrix Potter* (Frederick Warne & Co., London, 1946, repr 1985), p. 63.

42 Beatrix Potter to F. Warne & Co., 19 January 1902, BPL, p. 59.

Chapter 6

1 BPJ, 7 September 1885, p. 156.

2 BPJ, 18 June 1885, pp. 152–3.

3 Beatrix Potter to Norman Warne, 17 November 1904, BPL, p. 108.

4 BPJ, 11 October 1895, p. 407.

5 BPJ, 18 March 1885, p. 141.

6 BPJ, June 1894, p. 319.

7 Ibid.

8   Ibid., p. 320.

9   Ibid., p. 322.

10 Ibid., p. 320.

11 Ibid., p. 321.

12 Ibid., p. 326.

13 Lear, Linda, *Beatrix Potter: A Life in Nature* (Allen Lane, London, 2007), p. 157.

14 BPJ, 28 July 1896, p. 427.

15 Beatrix Potter to Norman Warne, 21 March 1903, BPL, p. 72.

16 Beatrix Potter to Norman Warne, 27 March 1903, BPL, p. 73.

17 Beatrix Potter to F. Warne & Co., 8 May 1902, BPL, p. 61.

18 Beatrix Potter to Norman Warne, 20 March 1903, BPL, p. 72.

19 Beatrix Potter to Norman Warne, 21 March 1903, BPL, p. 73.

20 Beatrix Potter to Millie Warne, 9 October 1910, BPL, p. 185.

21 Beatrix Potter to Norman Warne, 12 February 1904, BPL, p. 85.

22 Beatrix Potter to Fruing Warne, 7 October 1923, BPL, p. 283.

23 Beatrix Potter to Alexander McKay, 21 February 1929, BPL, p. 314.

24 Beatrix Potter to Norman Warne, 14 July 1903, BPL, p. 78.

25 Beatrix Potter to Norman Warne, 12 February 1904, BPL, p. 85.

26 Beatrix Potter to Norman Warne, 8 July 1903, BPL, p. 77.

27 Beatrix Potter to Norman Warne, 26 June 1905, BPL, p. 121.

28 Beatrix Potter to Norman Warne, 8 June 1905, BPL, p. 120.

29 Beatrix Potter to Norman Warne, 20 October 1904, BPL, p. 104.

30 Beatrix Potter to Millie Warne, 1 February 1906, BPL, p. 139.

31 Ibid.

32 Beatrix Potter to Norman Warne, ?September 1903, BPL, p. 81.

33 Beatrix Potter to Norman Warne, 12 February 1904, BPL, p. 85.

34 Beatrix Potter to Norman Warne, 1 March 1904, BPL, p. 88.

35 Beatrix Potter to Norman Warne, 9 November 1903, BPL, p. 82.

36 Beatrix Potter to Norman Warne, 15 December 1903, BPL, p. 84.

37 Beatrix Potter to Norman Warne, 12 November 1904, BPL, p. 107.

38 Lear, Linda, op. cit., p. 198.

39 Beatrix Potter to Harold Warne, 30 July 1905, BPL, p. 124.

40 Beatrix Potter, 13 August 1905, *Beatrix Potter: A Holiday Diary*, ed. Judy Taylor (The Beatrix Potter Society, London, 1996), p. 39.

41 Ibid., p. 13.

42 Ibid., 24 August 1905, p. 51.

43 Ibid., p. 52.

44 Ibid., p. 53.

45 BPJ, 6 September 1896, p. 432.

46 BPJ, 28 May 1895, p. 384.

47 Beatrix Potter to Winifred Warne, 6 September 1905, *Letters to Children from Beatrix Potter* (Frederick Warne & Co., London, 1992), collected and introduced by Judy Taylor, p. 121.

48 Beatrix Potter to Molly Gaddum, 11 October 1895, *Letters to Children*, op. cit., p. 98.

49 Lear, Linda, op. cit., p. 503.

50 *Beatrix Potter: A Holiday Diary*, op. cit., p. 58.

51 Beatrix Potter to Millie Warne, 22 August 1912, BPL, p. 199.

Chapter 7

1 Beatrix Potter to Bertha Mahony Miller, 25 November 1940, BPL, p. 423.

2 BPJ, 25 July 1896, p. 426.

3 BPJ, 23 July 1896, p. 426; 17 November 1896, p. 434.

4   BPJ, 26 July 1896, p. 426.

5   BPJ, 26 August 1896, p. 430.

6   BPJ, 28 July 1896, p. 427; 17 November 1896, p. 433.

7   BPJ, 17 November 1896, p. 433.

8   Beatrix Potter, *The Tale of Pigling Bland*, p. 69.

9   Beatrix Potter to Millie Warne, 14 October 1905, BPL, p. 134.

10 Beatrix Potter to Harold Warne, 10 October 1905, BPL, p. 133.

11 Lear, Linda, *Beatrix Potter: A Life in Nature* (Allen Lane, London, 2007), p. 496.

12 Hyde Parker, Ulla, *Cousin Beatie: A Memory of Beatrix Potter* (Frederick Warne & Co., London, 1981), p. 34.

13 Beatrix Potter to Millie Warne, 4 October 1906, BPL, p. 148.

14 Beatrix Potter to Harold Warne, 10 October 1905, BPL, p. 133.

15 *Beatrix Potter Studies IV* (The Beatrix Potter Society, London, 1990), p. 13.

16 Beatrix Potter to Louie Choyce, 15 March 1916, *The Choyce Letters*, ed. Judy Taylor (The Beatrix Potter Society, London, 1994), p. 12.

17 Beatrix Potter to Noel Moore, 17 April 1898; Beatrix Potter to Frida Moore, 26 January 1900, *Letters to Children from Beatrix Potter* (Frederick Warne & Co., London, 1992), collected and introduced by Judy Taylor, pp. 52, 64.

18 *Beatrix Potter's Americans: Selected Letters*, ed. Jane Crowell Morse (Horn Book, Boston, 1982), p. 207.

19 Beatrix Potter to Millie Warne, 18 July 1906, BPL, p. 142; Susan Denyer, *Beatrix Potter: At Home in the Lake District* (Frances Lincoln, London, 2000), p. 94.

20 Beatrix Potter to Norman Warne, 19 April 1904, BPL, p. 92.

21 Beatrix Potter to Harold Warne, 18 November 1908, BPL, p. 165.

22 Lane, Margaret, *The Tale of Beatrix Potter* (Frederick Warne & Co., London, 1946, repr 1985), p. 99; Beatrix Potter to Louisa Ferguson, 8 January 1910, *Letters to Children*, op. cit., p. 135.

23 Beatrix Potter to Harold Warne, 17 August 1908 and 15 December 1908, BPL, pp. 161, 166.

24 Beatrix Potter to Eileen Rowson, 6 March 1919, *Letters to Children*, op. cit., p. 191.

25 Beatrix Potter to Millie Warne, 17 November 1909, BPL, p. 171.

26 Beatrix Potter to Louie Warne, 6 July 1907 and 8 July 1907, *Letters to Children*, op. cit., pp. 123–4.

27 Beatrix Potter to Louie Choyce, 15 March 1916, *The Choyce Letters*, op. cit., p. 13.

28 Lear, Linda, op. cit., p. 236.

29 Taylor, Judy, *Beatrix Potter: Artist, Storyteller and Countrywoman* (Frederick Warne & Co., London, 1986), p. 120.

30 Beatrix Potter to Millie Warne, 6 October 1907, BPL, p. 155.

31 On jam-making, see Beatrix Potter to Louie Choyce, 15 March 1916, *The Choyce Letters*, op. cit., p. 14.

32 Beatrix Potter to Millie Warne, 6 October 1907, BPL, p. 155.

33 BPJ, 10 June 1884, p. 93.

34 Denyer, Susan, op. cit., p. 52.

35 Beatrix Potter to Louie Choyce, ?1925, *The Choyce Letters*, op. cit., p. 45.

36 Potter, Beatrix, *The Fairy Caravan* (Frederick Warne & Co., London, 1929, repr 1986), p. 40.

37 Beatrix Potter to Mrs J. Templeman Coolidge, 30 September 1927, BPL, p. 306.

38 Beatrix Potter to Louie Warne, 8 July 1907, BPL, p. 152.

39 Beatrix Potter to Hettie Douglas, 31 March 1939, BPL, p. 402.

40 Lear, Linda, op. cit., pp. 499, 239, 265.

41 Taylor, Judy, Whalley, Joyce Irene, et al., *Beatrix Potter 1866–1943: The Artist and Her World* (Frederick Warne & Co. with the National Trust, London, 1987), p. 135.

42 BPJ, 11 October 1895, p. 407.

43 Beatrix Potter to Louie Choyce, 25 May 1916, *The Choyce Letters*, op. cit., p. 17.

44 BPJ, 13 August 1896, p. 429.

45 *Beatrix Potter Studies IV* (The Beatrix Potter Society, London, 1990), p. 30.

46 De Vasconcelles, Josefina, *She was Loved: Memories of Beatrix Potter* (Titus Wilson, Kendal, 2003), p. 101.

47 Beatrix Potter to Margaret Hough, 4 November 1913, BPL, p. 214.

48 Hyde Parker, Ulla, *Cousin Beatie: A Memory of Beatrix Potter* (Frederick Warne & Co., London, 1981), p. 23.

49 Beatrix Potter to Andrew Fayle, c. 1909, *Letters to Children*, op. cit., p. 141.

50 Beatrix Potter to Andrew Fayle, 1909–10, ibid., p. 143.

51 Beatrix Potter to Augusta Burn, 25 August 1912, ibid., p. 158; Beatrix Potter to Millie Warne, 22 August 1912, BPL, p. 199.

52 Beatrix Potter to Harold Warne, 9 October 1912, BPL, p. 200.

53 Beatrix Potter to Caroline Clark, 15 February 1937, BPL, p. 384; Beatrix Potter to Louie Choyce, 15 March 1916, *The Choyce Letters*, op. cit., p. 13.

54 *Beatrix Potter Studies IV*, op. cit., p. 33.

55 Beatrix Potter to Augusta Burn, 31 December 1912, *Letters to Children*, op. cit., p. 159.

56 BPL, Beatrix Potter to Harold Warne, 3 March 1913 and 19 April 1913, BPL, pp. 203, 205.

57 Beatrix Potter to Millie Warne, 4 July 1913, Frederick Warne Archive.

58 Beatrix Potter to Margaret Hough, 4 November 1913, BPL, p. 214.

CHAPTER 8

1   Hyde Parker, Ulla, *Cousin Beatie: A Memory of Beatrix Potter* (Frederick Warne & Co., London, 1981), p. 23.
2   Beatrix Potter to Barbara Buxton, 31 December 1913, BPL, p. 215.
3   BPJ, 5 June 1891, p. 217.
4   Beatrix Potter to Millie Warne, 30 September 1906, 14 October 1905 and 5 April 1906, BPL, pp. 146, 134, 140.
5   Hyde Parker, Ulla, op. cit., p. 21.
6   Lear, Linda, *Beatrix Potter: A Life in Nature* (Allen Lane, London, 2007), p. 343
7   Beatrix Potter to Henry P. Coolidge, 28 June 1928, *Letters to Children from Beatrix Potter* (Frederick Warne & Co., London, 1992), collected and introduced by Judy Taylor, p. 216.
8   Ibid., p. 212.
9   Beatrix Potter to Harold Warne, 23 February 1914, BPL, p. 216.
10 Beatrix Potter to Harold Warne, 12 July 1914, BPL, p. 218.
11 Beatrix Potter to Edith Gaddum, 8 June 1923, BPL, p. 282.
12 Lear, Linda, op. cit., p. 235.
13 Beatrix Potter to Harold Warne, 9 May 1914, BPL, p. 217.
14 *Beatrix Potter Studies IV* (The Beatrix Potter Society, London, 1990), p. 38.
15 Lear, Linda, op. cit., p. 366.
16 Beatrix Potter to Harold Warne, 12 July 1914, BPL, p. 218.
17 Beatrix Potter to William Warner, 11 August 1908, private collection.
18 BPJ, 8 August 1895, p. 392.
19 BPJ, 17 August 1895, p. 395.

NOTES

20 Beatrix Potter to Louie Choyce, 15 March 1916, *The Choyce Letters*, ed. Judy Taylor (The Beatrix Potter Society, London, 1994), p. 12.

21 Beatrix Potter to Harold Warne, 18 May 1915, BPL, p. 221.

22 Beatrix Potter to Harold Warne, 12 August 1916, and Beatrix Potter to Ernest A. Aris, 23 November 1917, BPL, pp. 227, 241.

23 Beatrix Potter to Bertha Mahony Miller, 25 November 1940, BPL, p. 423.

24 Beatrix Potter to Millie Warne, 15 December 1916, BPL, p. 228.

25 Beatrix Potter to Harold Warne, 3 August 1914, BPL, p. 219.

26 Beatrix Potter to Fruing Warne, ?18 December 1915, BPL, p. 222.

27 Ibid., 4 May 1918, BPL, p. 247.

28 Taylor, Judy, op. cit., p. 138.

29 Beatrix Potter to Fruing Warne, 17 October 1917, BPL, p. 238.

30 Ibid., 21 June 1917, BPL, p. 234; Beatrix Potter to Tom Harding, 21 December 1917, *Letters to Children*, op. cit., p. 180.

31 Beatrix Potter to Fruing Warne, 17 October 1917, BPL, p. 238.

32 Ibid., 28 February 1919, BPL, p. 254.

33 Beatrix Potter to Fruing Warne, 12 January 1921, BPL, p. 267.

34 Ibid., 3 November 1919, BPL, p. 259.

35 Beatrix Potter to Sylvie Heelis, 17 September 1921, BPL, p. 273.

36 Beatrix Potter to Miss Wyatt, 15 November 1920, BPL, p. 264.

37 Beatrix Potter to Sylvie Heelis, 29 July 1922, and Beatrix Potter to Bruce Thompson, BPL, pp. 279 and 349.

38 BPJ, 23 April 1883, p. 38.

39 Beatrix Potter to Tom Harding, 21 December 1917, *Letters to Children*, op. cit., p. 180.

40 Beatrix Potter to Esther Nicholson, 16 July 1918, *Letters to Children*, p. 175.

41 Beatrix Potter to Neville Rowson, 6 March 1919, *Letters to Children*, p. 192.

42 Lear, Linda, op. cit., pp. 290, 390.

43 Beatrix Potter to Louie Choyce, 15 March 1916, *The Choyce Letters*, op. cit., p. 12.

44 Beatrix Potter to Bertha Mahony Miller, 13 December 1934, BPL, p. 371.

CHAPTER 9

1 BPJ, 26 May 1884, p. 89.

2 Ibid.

3 BPJ, 9 September 1895, p. 400.

4 Potter, Beatrix, *The Fairy Caravan* (Frederick Warne & Co., London, 1929, repr 1986), p. 178.

5 *Beatrix Potter Studies IV* (The Beatrix Potter Society, London, 1990), p. 44.

6 Beatrix Potter to Millie Warne, 13 December 1911; Beatrix Potter to the editor of *Country Life* (published 13 January 1912), BPL, pp. 192-3.

7 Beatrix Potter to Bertha Mahony, 20 May 1927, BPL, p. 304.

8 Beatrix Potter to Harold Warne, 8 January 1910, BPL, pp. 174-5.

9 Beatrix Potter, *The Fairy Caravan*, op. cit., p. 130.

10 Beatrix Potter to Alexander McKay, 20 February 1929, BPL, p. 313.

11 Beatrix Potter to Henry P. Coolidge, 1 January 1930, BPL, pp. 328-9.

12 Denyer, Susan, *Beatrix Potter: At Home in the Lake District* (Frances Lincoln, London, 2000), p. 124.

13 Ibid., p. 120.

14 Lear, Linda, *Beatrix Potter: A Life in Nature* (Allen Lane, London, 2007), p. 9.

15 *Beatrix Potter Studies IV*, op. cit., p. 54.

16 Ibid., p. 44.

17 Beatrix Potter to Mr D. M. Matheson, 17 October 1939, BPL, p. 410.

18 BPJ, 18 October 1892, p. 295.

19 Beatrix Potter to Mr S. H. Hamer, 20 October 1929, BPL, p. 318; Taylor, Judy, op. cit., p. 180.

20 Beatrix Potter to John Stone, 5 June 1940, BPL, p. 416.

21 Hyde Parker, Ulla, *Cousin Beatie: A Memory of Beatrix Potter* (Frederick Warne & Co., London, 1981), p. 23.

22 Ibid., p. 15.

23 Taylor, Judy, *Beatrix Potter: Artist, Storyteller and Countrywoman* (Frederick Warne & Co., London, 1986), p. 175.

24 Beatrix Potter to Daisy Hammond and Cecily Mills, 30 March 1939, BPL, p. 398.

25 Taylor, Judy, op. cit., p. 185.

26 Ibid., p. 190.

27 Ibid., p. 203.

28 Beatrix Potter to Bertha Mahony Miller, 18 June 1942, BPL, p. 449.

29 Beatrix Potter to Mrs J. Templeman Coolidge, 9 December 1929, BPL, p. 324.

30 *Beatrix Potter Studies IV*, op. cit., p. 47.

31 Ibid., p. 41.

32 Denyer, Susan, op. cit., p. 137.

33 *Beatrix Potter Studies IV*, op. cit., p. 40.

34 Beatrix Potter to June Steel, 11 October 1939, BPL, p. 408.

35 Taylor, Judy, op. cit., p. 190.

36 Beatrix Potter to Nora Burt, 5 June 1931, BPL, p. 341.

37 Carpenter, Humphrey, *Secret Gardens: A Study of the Golden Age of Children's Literature* (Allen & Unwin, London, 1985), p. 141.

38 Beatrix Potter to Caroline Clark, 15 February 1937, BPL, p. 384.

39 Taylor, Judy, op. cit., p. 191.

40 Denyer, Susan, op. cit., p. 103.

41 Beatrix Potter to Henry P. Coolidge, 28 June 1928, *Letters to Children*, op. cit., p. 215.

AFTERWORD

1 BPJ, 28 May 1895, p. 387; Beatrix Potter to Arthur Stephens, 12 May 1942, BPL, p. 444; Linder, Leslie, *A History of the Writings of Beatrix Potter, including Unpublished Work* (Frederick Warne & Co., London, 1971), p. 357.

2 Beatrix Potter to Noel Moore, 4 June 1895, *Letters to Children from Beatrix Potter* (Frederick Warne & Co., London, 1992), collected and introduced by Judy Taylor, p. 32.

3 BPJ, 22 September 1892, p. 273.

4 Beatrix Potter to Josephine Banner, 28 February 1938, BPL, p. 387.

5 BPJ, 5 June 1891, p. 217.

6 Beatrix Potter to Sylvie Heelis, 17 September 1921, BPL, p. 272.

7 Beatrix Potter to Henry P. Coolidge, 28 June 1928, BPL, p. 311.

8 Hyde Parker, Ulla, *Cousin Beatie: A Memory of Beatrix Potter* (Frederick Warne & Co., London, 1981), p. 23.

List of Illustrations

p. 1 Beatrix Potter, aged five (The Beatrix Potter Society; www.beatrixpottersociety.org.uk).

p. 21 Portrait of a young Beatrix Potter (The Beatrix Potter Society; www.beatrixpottersociety.org.uk).

p. 49 Beatrix and Bertram Potter (The Beatrix Potter Society; www.beatrixpottersociety.org.uk).

p. 77 Beatrix Potter at Dalguise (Popperfoto / Getty Images).

p. 101 Beatrix Potter with Benjamin H. Bouncer (© WorldPhotos / Alamy Stock Photo).

p. 125 Beatrix Potter, aged twenty-six, in Birnham, Scotland (Hulton Archive / Getty Images).

p. 153 Beatrix Potter in the porch at Hill Top (Topfoto).

p. 181 Beatrix Potter with William Heelis, 1913 (Courtesy of a private collector).

p. 201 Beatrix Potter with Tom Storey (Beatrix Potter Gallery © National Trust / Robert Thrift).

Plates

Coloured sketch of foxgloves (courtesy of the Trustees of the Linder Collection).

Unfinished painting of the interior of Melford Hall, 1903 (courtesy of the Trustees of the Linder Collection).

Amanitopsis vaginata by Beatrix Potter, from a specimen found at Keswick, 30 August 1897 (courtesy of the Armitt Trust, Ambleside).

'A view over hills and valleys' by Beatrix Potter (courtesy of the Trustees of the Linder Collection).

'The Meal' from 'The Rabbits' Christmas Party' (courtesy of the Victoria and Albert Museum).

'Come dance a jig to my Granny's pig' (courtesy of the Victoria and Albert Museum).

'The Mice Listen to the Tailor's Lament' from *The Tailor of Gloucester* (courtesy of Tate Images).

Water lilies on Esthwaite Water (courtesy of the Victoria and Albert Museum).

Index

INDEX